More Critical Praise for
Steidlmayer on Markets, Second Edition

"It is a well known fact that Pete Steidlmayer codified the Market Profile and presented it to the world. In terms of applying the profile to real-time trading, no one has more insight than Steve Hawkins. If you want to understand the nuances of market behavior and what it takes to be a great trader, then you had better buy this book."

Gerard de Condappa
Floor Trader
SIMEX
Former Member of CBOT & Mid-America Futures Exchanges

"*Steidlmayer on Markets* is a technically proficient, insightful, and thoroughly educational read. . . . And today's challenging financial markets require innovative and dynamic analysis such as 'market profile'. For the financial market novice or professional trader *Steidlmayer on Markets* should be on the list of required reading materials."

Joseph Stewart
Global Head IR/FX Technical Strategy
UBS Warburg

"An important and comprehensible update on an intriguing system. I don't know of any magic bullets in trading, but this system definitely provides an edge. It offers a tremendous amount of information on what the market is doing, the more time and energy you put into it, the more you get out of it."

Josh Stiles
New York Research Director and Senior Strategist
IDEAglobal

Founded in 1807, John Wiley & Sons is the oldest independent publishing company in the United States. With offices in North America, Europe, Australia, and Asia, Wiley is globally committed to developing and marketing print and electronic products and services for our customers' professional and personal knowledge and understanding.

The Wiley Trading series features books by traders who have survived the market's ever-changing temperament and have prospered—some by reinventing systems, others by getting back to basics. Whether a novice trader, professional, or somewhere in-between, these books will provide the advice and strategies needed to prosper today and well into the future.

For a list of available titles, please visit our Web site at www.WileyFinance.com.

Steidlmayer on Markets
Trading with Market Profile

Second Edition

J. Peter Steidlmayer

Steven B. Hawkins

John Wiley & Sons, Inc.

Hoboken • Chichester • Weinheim • Brisbane • Singapore • Toronto

Published by John Wiley & Sons, Inc., Hoboken, New Jersey
Published simultaneously in Canada

For general information on our other products and services, or technical support, please
contact our Customer Care Department within the United States at 800-762-2974, outside the United States at 317-572-3993, or fax 317-572-4002.

Wiley also publishes its books in a variety of electronic formats. Some content that appears in print may not be available in electronic books.

Library of Congress Cataloging-in-Publication Data:

ISBN 0-471-21556-2

10 9 8 7 6 5 4 3 2

FOREWORD

A chart is a communication vehicle. Its purpose is to communicate what is transpiring at point A (trading pit) to an observer at point B (some distant location). One can look at any charting system (e.g., bar, point and figure, candlestick) as a language. Each was developed to communicate market condition to an observer. The language of trading has its own vernacular. Examples include: "it feels heavy here," or "it feels like we have more to go." Market Profile is the product of a professional floor trader's ability to communicate the pit trading experience symbolically in chart form. Here is how this is accomplished.

The standard 30-minute bar chart automatically moves to the right to start a new bar every 30 minutes. The horizontal dimension in this chart is automatic—dictated by chronological time, not market activity. The involuntary nature of this action inhibits the ability of the bar chart to communicate market activity in the horizontal. This limitation is analogous to trying to communicate detail or nuance using only nouns and verbs but no adjectives or adverbs—less than adequate communication.

Market Profile has no chronological restriction. It expands horizontally only when prices repeat. Horizontal expansion of the chart reflects only market activity, never chronological activity (the passage of time). Market Profile more clearly illustrates to the trader a new directional move beginning in a dead market or a directional move losing momentum. The feel of the market is objectively illustrated using the horizontal dimension.

Visual focus = Accurate communication = Better trade identification

Jim Mayer—President
Mayer Investments

ACKNOWLEDGMENTS

First of all, I would like to thank Pete Steidlmayer for the opportunity to work on this book. He has been a tremendous mentor, and has offered direction, yet allowed me to stumble, bumble, and make mistakes along the way, all of which are necessary in the learning process. His vote of confidence in my understanding of this methodology is greatly appreciated.

Second, the sacrifices of my wife, Jackie; and children, Steven, Nicole, Joshua, and Bennett have in general been unacknowledged yet not unappreciated. Without their support, understanding, and encouragement, this work wouldn't have been possible.

And lastly, I would like to thank all those who have supported me during my professional career as well as those involved in my early life development. They helped lay the foundation for my future and helped me understand the need for balance in one's life.

Steven B. Hawkins
October 2002

CONTENTS

I   The Steidlmayer Method 1

Chapter 1   Early Lessons 3
Trust and Freedom 3
The Importance of Fixing the Gate 5
The Secrets of Order and Control 6
Looking Beyond the Self 7
Glimpses of Markets at Work 8

Chapter 2   College Years 15
The Markets Beckon 15
Discovering the Bell Curve 17
John Schultz and the Minimum Trend 19
Charting the Minimum Trend 21

Chapter 3   Chicago 29
False Start 29
Breaking In 30
Success in a Responsive Market 32
Learning by Observation 33
Exposure, Excesses, and the Long- and Short-Term Trader 33
The Common Laws of the Market Place 35

Chapter 4   Changing Markets 37
The Advent of Commodity Trading Funds 37
The 1970s: Greater Markets, Greater Opportunities 40
Narrow-Range Days and New Activity 41

Chapter 5   The Information Revolution **43**
   Opening Up the Market 43
   Price Recurrence and Volume 44
   The Natural Organization of the Market—Revealed 44
   Fundamental and Technical Information 46

II   The Hawkins Interpretation **49**

Chapter 6   Understanding Market Profile **51**
   Basic Principles of Market Profile 56
   Reading the Market Profile Chart 57
   Day Structures: Five Typical Patterns 59
   Four Steps of Market Activity 70
   Internal Time Clock of the Market 73
   Timeslots-Used Matrix 75
   Beyond-The-Day Activity 82
   Initiating Versus Responsive Activity 89
   Excesses 92
   Market Profile and Spreads 92

Chapter 7   Liquidity Data Bank, On Floor Information,
   and Volume @ Time **97**
   Understanding the Liquidity Data Bank Report 98
   Understanding On Floor Information 101
   Understanding Volume @ Time 106
   Steps in Interpreting the Liquidity Data Bank Report 108
   Steps in Interpreting On Floor Information 113
   Steps in Interpreting Volume @ Time 114
   Blow Off Extreme 115
   Volume Excess 117
   Zero Line 122

Chapter 8   The Steidlmayer Theory of Markets **125**
   The Market 125
   Is an Organized Medium 126
   That Expresses Human Behavior 127
   In Different Price Areas at a Given Point in Time 127
   Always Presenting an Opportunity to Someone 128

Chapter 9   The Steidlmayer Distribution **131**
   Purpose of Market 131
   The Normal Distribution Versus the Steidlmayer Distribution 132
   Illustrating the Steidlmayer Distribution 134
   The Steidlmayer Distribution and Speed of Market Movement 137

Chapter 10   The You **139**
   Objectivity 139
   Market Discipline 141

Chapter 11   Anatomy of a Trade **145**
   Game Plan 146
   Trade Setups 151
   Human Capacity 153
   Volume Studies 154
   Utilizing a Chronological Data Base 158
   Trading Parallel Activity 159
   Trading Day Structure 163
   Auction Points and Single Prints 168
   Background Versus Foreground 176
   Creating a High Level of Trading 176

Chapter 12   Profile of the Successful Trader **181**

Chapter 13   Trading, Technology, and the Future **185**
   Long-term Capital 185
   Market Profile Display 186
   Market Time 189
   Auto Splitter 191
   Focused Output 194
   Proprietary Studies 195
   Lonesome Dove/Other Studies 198
   Product Creation 198
   Capflow32 201
   What is Access? 203
   MD_Trader 205
   Other Access Options 211

Endnotes **215**

Index **217**

Steidlmayer on Markets
Trading with Market Profile

Second Edition

Section I

The Steidlmayer Method

Chapter 1

EARLY LESSONS

The most important element in becoming a successful trader is having a sound background consisting of a strong base of knowledge acquired from being active in the markets through time. Building this background is in some ways the easiest and in other ways the most difficult thing for a trader to accomplish. Trading experiences, observations of all kinds, a focus on what is most important, and a clear understanding of business principles are all necessary ingredients in a strong trading background. Awareness and patience are also required to further develop one's background. Without a sound background, one's trading cannot be consistently successful. With it, one can develop clear, correct ways of thinking and confidence in one's trading judgment. In today's fast-moving world, some traders try to bypass the crucial first step of developing a sound background, and then rationalize the lack of background for the rest of their careers.

But the opportunity to develop the needed background is always there. I would like to share the background that underlies my own understanding of the markets. The experiences that went into building it are varied and required a lot of time and hard work. If you can learn the principles that these experiences illustrate, you will find that the same principles figure in your own experiences as a trader. I think you will also learn some things about today's markets.

Trust and Freedom

In my formative years, from 1944 until I completed high school in 1956, I gained both education and knowledge. Education provides a foundation and method for learning, but knowledge comes through experience. Thus, a lot of knowledge develops on a subconscious level. I was not aware of this subconscious learning process when I was growing up, but in later years I found that I had a large storehouse of knowledge to draw on to gain a good understanding of any subject. I had stored in my subconscious a database of real knowledge that came from varied experiences.

I grew up on a ranch in California and much of my early learning came from being exposed to the family business. Skill was greatly respected in my family, but more important than skill was integrity. People who were disloyal, dishonest, or untrustworthy were not needed regardless of how skilled they might be. If my family was doing business with someone who turned out to be untrustworthy, we stopped doing business with him or her no matter how rewarding the deal might appear to be on an immediate basis. We used this principle to avoid major losses in the future, and I stick by this principle to this day.

In my family, no one was condemned for making mistakes. We understood that all knowledge came from making mistakes. This idea became dominant as I ventured out into the world and got bumped occasionally. "That was a good experience," my parents would say. "Learn from it and go forward."

My parents did not criticize or analyze the mistakes we boys made. We did that on our own. The burden of facing up to our mistakes and learning from each experience was on our shoulders. Patience was always stressed because it reflected and developed our inner self-confidence. We were not expected to show quick results; it was understood that "slow and steady wins the race."

My parents encouraged me to take my time to find a profession that I enjoyed rather than one they would like me to pursue. The object was to do things and to find out what I could and could not do—then I would be able to make choices for the future. Later I learned about the American Indian practice of putting a young man of 11 or 12 years old out alone on a mountaintop or in the desert to spend several days searching for the meaning of his life. The revelation might come through a sign or perhaps through a dream. Either might reveal the young man's destined path. I was raised in the same spirit, and it has become an important part of my background as a trader.

Home was a base from which we could venture and a sanctuary to which we could always return. My parents assured us that we would always be welcome to stay with them no matter how bad things were. But we were responsible to ourselves, to those surrounding us, and to the community. If we ever violated that trust, we might lose our sanctuary. Success was viewed as temporary. We were encouraged not to get too excited when things went well or too depressed when things did not, but to remain emotionally balanced. Time was the most important measurement of all. A person or an idea had to stand the test of time. New ideas and dreams were not disregarded, even if they did not work out. They were considered opportunities for learning and growth.

The Importance of Fixing the Gate

When I worked for my father, I learned not to run away from a problem and to finish what I started. Our philosophy was to do the job once and do it right. My father never understood why people would fail to recognize a problem or, if they did, why they would not deal with it unless forced to. We had many wooden gates on our ranch, and from time to time they would need repair. When our ranch hands went through a broken gate, they would open and close it without stopping to fix it. By contrast, my father would fix the gate then and there. That was his way.

Years later, when the markets changed in 1969, the trading method I had developed no longer worked—it was "broken." Although I was trading in the markets every day, I did not want to face the reality of the broken gate. Once I realized that I was running away from the problem, just as the ranch hands had ignored the broken gate, I motivated myself to stop and correct the problem. I also learned from my father the importance of the last 10 percent of any job. He always said that this was the most important part of any task—the part that required the greatest discipline. This final effort separates success from failure; it separates the person who always has 10 projects 90 percent done from the person who successfully finishes each task. It separates the many climbers who reach the 25,000-foot level on Everest from the few who reach the summit.

The same philosophy applies to trading. The willingness to follow through on a task marks the difference between those who are almost successful and those who achieve their goals. In my family, we also learned to recognize the abilities of others. Some people have more talent than you, others less. Do not compete outside yourself; try to be the best you can within your own abilities. But learn from observing yourself and the many types of people around you.

The Secrets of Order and Control

In August 1946, when I was 7 years old, my father and I were moving a tractor from our valley ranch to our ranch in Nevada. As we reached the foothills around 4 P.M., about 4 hours from our destination, we got a flat tire and stopped at a tire shop in Orville, California. In those days, truck tires were complicated to take apart and put back together, so at about 4:50 they were still working on it. My father was anxious to get on with the trip. The mechanic wanted to quit work at 5:00, so both men wanted to get the job done. I watched them take the tire apart trying to put it together again and again, emotionally beating at the tire with a hammer and swearing at it. Finally, I piped up, "Why don't you put the tire back together the opposite way you took it apart?" I can still see the mechanic's face as he turned his head toward me—his face covered with dirt and sweat—and said, "Well, how is that, sonny?" I proceeded to tell him how, and 5 minutes later we were on our way.

I learned that by watching you could perceive a sense of order. Emotions and impatience do not produce results—observation and understanding do. I have found the same to be true in trading. When working the land, there was pride in the different chores we were given. A job had to be done according to standards that were acceptable to our parents and to the ranch. More importantly, it had to meet our own standards first, before we even showed anyone the completed job. In my family, your job was you—a reflection of your standards. The full-time ranch workers did a good job with the income-producing crops, but not as well with the fill-in jobs, which kept them occupied during slack times. One of these jobs was irrigating the back pasture. You could not get water across the back pasture because it had never been leveled. If you were irrigating a bean or corn crop, which was planted on level ground, you were expected to make sure water got over every inch. But everybody slacked off on the fill-in jobs because no one ever checked them. But when I was asked to irrigate the back pasture, I designed a system of dams to get water all over the field, which had never before been fully irrigated. No one ever knew, but that did not matter because I got personal satisfaction out of doing it. I realized that if I stayed within the accepted standards for the job, I would not learn anything. By stretching myself beyond the standards, forcing myself to do more, I learned a lot.

Another experience taught me to have confidence in my abilities and to take control of a situation. I was riding with our dogs on the back edge of a trailer that my dad was pulling behind the pickup truck. We were moving down a rugged road at about 25 miles an hour. Suddenly, the trailer hit a bumpy stretch of the road, and I realized that I could not hang on because there was no place to grip on the back of the trailer. I pictured myself falling off the truck onto the rocky road. I could see that if I fell, I would probably break my arms and possibly die. I panicked. I started to scream, and the dogs began to bark, but my dad could not hear over the noise of the pickup and the rattle of the bounding trailer.

Fortunately, I figured out a way to avoid disaster. By lifting my body off the truck with my arms and tilting my weight back toward my head, I was able to absorb the bounce in my arms and keep my balance. I rode that way for about three-quarters of a mile, until we got to the shop. I never told my father about this experience, although I had been really scared by it. I learned not to accept disaster. In this episode I fought off disaster with my brains and my muscles and I gained confidence in my own abilities as a result.

Looking Beyond the Self

One Saturday when I was about 11, I wanted to hunt ducks. It was a rainy day with a strong south wind, and there were ducks and geese all over the ranch. My brothers and I had to move about 1,500 sheep from one ranch to another before I could go hunting. My father warned me not to cut across the fields with the sheep. But as we proceeded, I grew more and more anxious to go hunting because we were passing right by the ducks and geese. Finally, I told my brothers that we should take the sheep across the field to get to the other ranch faster. As we approached the middle of the field, about 150 sheep got stuck in the mud. If you can image 150 sheep up to their bellies in mud—each weighing more than I did—you know what we were dealing with.

Normally the ranch hands got off at noon on Saturdays, but not that week. Everyone worked until 3 P.M. pulling sheep out of the mud—I was too small to move them myself. No one complained, but I realized that my selfish interest had given a lot of people a lot of extra work. From that experience I learned not to put myself first.

To me, success in trading also requires unselfishness. When you are in the pit, you have an obligation to other traders and brokers in the pit to contribute to the well-being of the marketplace, not just to seek your own profit. The marketplace comes before you or any other individual trader.

Glimpses of Markets at Work

Observing the ranch hands trading in used guns and cars and my father trading in land, equipment, and crops taught me to take advantage of situations rather than letting them take advantage of me. At harvest time, my father was not speculating for big gains. Hc wanted a fair price for his crop to make a normal profit for his work and his capital investment. If the price at harvest time was fair, he sold. If he felt the price was not fair, he held and stored the grain.

When buying, my father wanted a fair price as well. I remember going with my father shopping to buy all the groceries for the camp. He knew the price of everything, and he always bought sale items. If the price was too high he would not buy; he would substitute or go without. He had a list of what he thought each item should cost, and he would check off the list when he got to the counter to make sure they did not make any mistakes in adding up the bill.

When my father had the option of buying some used farm equipment, he behaved just as the ranch workers did when they were buying a used car. If the car was undervalued, they would buy it; if it was overvalued, they would not. At the cattle sales, my father would say, "You can make a lot of money just being a sharp buyer. But if you overpay, there's no way to get it back." I learned that if you pay more than fair value for something, time is against you; but if you underpay, time is on your side. This became the underpinning of my approach to trading commodities.

My father had one rule in buying property: 6 months or a year after you buy the property, your neighbor should be willing to pay what you paid for it. That was his measurement of value. He was an optimistic man, but one imprinted by the experience of the Depression. Although he went out of his way to avoid debt, he could see that in the postwar world values were changing, making it necessary to use debt judiciously. He knew that the focus of the ranch should not be on daily operations, but on land acquisitions. So he would never borrow to finance daily operations, but he would use credit to buy land.

In buying property, my father had different time frames, different needs, and different motives, depending on the situation. He once planned to buy a ranch with his brothers at an auction. It was a sealed-bid auction, at which everybody had the right to raise the bid 10 percent. On our way to the auction, he told me that the other people there would have more money than he did and that he would have to scare them out of the auction if he hoped to get the land. To do so, he bid a lot higher than what people thought the land was worth so there would not be any after-auction rebids.

When his bid was announced, a hush fell over the crowd. Many of the farmers in the area told my father that they would sell him their land at that price. No one else tried to raise the bid, and my father accomplished his goal. A good broker or trader does the same thing. Many times, they use a higher-than-normal price to attract traders, realizing that in the short term they were overpaying, but later that price would be a good one.

In another instance, my father acquired a piece of property by playing a waiting game. He felt that nobody else was going to buy the property so he had plenty of time. The attorney for the estate dickered over the price for a year and a half, but my father knew that the estate had to sell it. He gambled on the chance that no one else would buy it, and he won. He got the property for about 40 percent less than the original asking price. Again, the relationship of market conditions to value and to the buyer's and seller's needs was critical. My father was always prepared. He always had a game plan.

When he started ranching back in 1916, he knew what he was going to buy and how he was going to accomplish his plan. He had the patience to do it over time. He knew when to move quickly and when to move slowly. I was always after him to buy other pieces of property that were outside his game plan. But he never would. He always refused to buy marginal properties because he felt that he should never buy anything bad or sell anything good.

My father explained these ideas to me, and although I had had no previous market experiences of my own, I began to see the difference between buying a used car, buying a gun, buying a piece of land, or selling crops. These were all different markets, and depending on the needs of the individual, there were different ways to approach each market applying the same principles of value to different conditions.

There was a wool buyer who came up from Stockton, California, to buy the tag ends of the pelts and the wool that was not sold at shearing. My father noticed that every time the buyer came up, the wool market would pick up. He asked the wool buyer about this and Mr. S. explained, "That's what I'm in business for." This was the first inkling I had that markets could be read and understood. My father was aware that Mr. S. had a deadline from which he was operating. The wool market was active only a couple of times a year. If my father did not sell his wool to Mr. S. within the deadline, he would miss the opportunity to sell. He also noticed that the frequency of the wool buyer's phone calls and visits would increase as his deadline approached.

My father used to trap skunks and raccoons along the river, dry the pelts, and sell them for Christmas money. Mr. S. would come up to our ranch in November and pay a big price for these ratty pelts, as a loss leader to get my dad in a good mood. He would also make a low offer for the wool to be sheared later in the year. My dad would naturally refuse to sell the wool at this low price.

Mr. S. would call again in a month or so with a higher price and would continue to call more and more frequently until the deal was struck. I watched my father play his different prices and frequency of contact off against the deadline for selling the wool in an active market. In this way, an amicable deal in which both people made money was eventually struck. My father always said that both sides had to make money for any deal to succeed. Whenever my father sold wool, cattle, sheep or any other commodity, he felt that the information about the sale was between him and the buyer, and that others who might be interested had no right to the information. So I learned early that transactional data are more important information in any market than nominal quotes. (Nominal quotes are bid and offer prices, representing the general parameters of what a price could be. They are not necessarily confirmed by an actual transaction. Data from a real transaction are much more meaningful.) By being active in the marketplace, you gain information. This has held true throughout my trading career. The more active I am as a trader, the more information I have in my hand.

As a child, my only business deal involving land occurred when I was 16. My mother had 10 acres on the outskirts of Colusa, California, on which a normal farming profit would be about $20 an acre per year. But the parcel was not large enough to merit farming. A company with a contract to run a power line across the valley wanted this high ground next to Highway 20 as a storage area for its trucks, towers, and equipment because much of the rest of the county was flooded with water in the winter. They offered us $75 rental for one acre of the parcel for a year. My mother thought that was a good offer, but I said I could get her $1,000. I remember my dad saying, "It's your choice, Mother. You can take a sure $75 or you can take Pete's promise of $1,000."

The next day my mother decided to go with me. I met the power company representative in the afternoon and told him what we got for similar properties. I explained that there were fairgrounds across from the property and that if we rented it to his company, we would not be able to get the parking revenues we usually received. This was a slight exaggeration. A fair was held every year across the road and people did park on our property, but we had never received any payment for this. To compensate, we wanted $1,000 for the acre.

The representative said he would talk to his home office and let us know. Three or 4 days later he accepted the deal. I felt that I had done a good job and created a deal that was fair to both sides. The power company ended up staying for 3 years. My mother made $3,000 instead of $225, and I received a 5 percent commission.

To my father, $75 cash represented real value, while I could see that the value of the land to the power company representative far exceeded $1,000. He needed to be close to the road and to be able to use the high property while the rest of the county was flooded in the winter. So the market worked in this case to find a fair price. It moved up quickly from $75 to $1,000 because it was undervalued at $75.

It also may have been undervalued at $1,000. We do not know because there was no other comparable reference point. I did not ask a price high enough to evoke a lower counter offer. So to this day, we do not know for sure whether the $1,000 price was really a good deal or not. I was satisfied at the time, but maybe I could have done better.

My father believed that it is very difficult to get ahead and be successful. He always said that the main thing is to be consistently good over a long period of time. Play the compound interest game. Build your base slowly and surely. A small increase on a big base is better than a big move on no base.

The key in business is to make sure that you win in the long run and that you can sustain yourself on the down side. If you can handle the downs, you'll always be successful—that was my father's theory. This same principle has worked as part of my trading strategy.

My mother was more of a general guide for me. She would say, "Go out and do things. You can't learn without experience." Her point was that when you go beyond your knowledge base, you are not going to be successful immediately, but you will gain experience that expands your base and ultimately propels you forward. I came to realize that, like everyone else, I was surrounded by a big bubble that kept me close to my family, my economic base, and my community. I became convinced that I had to move outside that bubble to be successful. I respected my community and its values, but I had to set myself apart from the goals and aspirations of others. This realization set the stage for the next phase of my development.

Chapter 2

COLLEGE YEARS

In 1957, I decided to go to college. I wanted to break with the strong social tradition that you had to go to college to do things. But I finally enrolled as an accounting major at the University of California at Berkeley because I wanted to see what college was like. I knew that I was not going to work for anybody else, and that the grades I got in school were not going to make much difference to me. I just wanted the experience of college. If I found that there was no benefit for me, I was not going to stay. As far as I was concerned, there would be no stigma about leaving.

The Markets Beckon

My first experience with organized markets came at Berkeley during 1957 and 1958. There was a recession in the economy, but stock prices were rallying. Friends of mine were doing quite well with their stock holdings, and I became intrigued and started to watch the market. I noticed the contrast between economic forecasts and what actually happened. I believe it was in the spring of 1958 that an article appeared in *Fortune* magazine about a father and son team of commodity traders. They started out with $10,000 and made more than a million trading before losing almost all of it and ending up with a $20,000 or $30,000 profit after commissions. I was amazed that so much money could be made in a short time from such a small starting base. I began to read about the commodity markets and follow them. I got recommendations on trading corn, wheat, soybeans, and soybean oil from various brokerage houses. I started trading but I was unsuccessful. I inherited $500 from my grandfather, who died at the age of 99, and I lost it all in 1 day. That was sobering. It took my grandfather 99 years to save that money, and I blew it in a day. Fortunately, I did not have any more money to lose. In all my early learning experiences, my trading stake was never more than $500 or $600. So this part of my education was not expensive.

During the summer of 1958, my father and my uncles decided that my cousins and I could farm some double crop land (wheat followed by beans) and use the earnings to fund our college educations. I had a dream that by planting the crop at the end of June and harvesting it in October, I was going to make $25,000. To do this, everything had to work perfectly. I would need a big crop and a high price.

As the summer progressed, I kept refiguring my expenses and my revenues, and I kept lowering my expected profit—down to $15,000, and $10,000. When I figured that it was only $6,000, I harvested the beans and got a roadside bid of 10 cents a pound. I laughed at the bid and said that I wanted 17 cents a pound—the price beans had traded at the year before. I watched as the price went from 10.25 cents to 10 cents to 9.75 cents, and so on, down in quarter-cent increments to 6.50 cents in December. Only because I had had a good yield could the 6.50 cents price allow me to repay my bank loan. I ended up with nothing for myself.

After I sold the beans at 6.50 cents. I watched them go up to about 14 cents per pound by the following April or May. I was very fortunate that I had not had much money to lose. I had been able to stop my losses at zero, which a lot of people in the commodities business cannot do.

Many commodity traders go through experiences like the one I had that summer. My plan had been based on a totally unrealistic idea—a set of dreams and hopes rather than facts. When a trade is developed this way, you are generally forced to exit it at the bottom of the move and you are unable to take advantage of any price rise that follows. Your trade may really have been right, but you lacked the knowledge, experience, and discipline to pull it off.

Discovering the Bell Curve

I had my first awakening in the spring of 1958, when I took a statistics course at Berkeley and was introduced to the concept of the bell curve. For those not familiar with statistics or the bell curve, Figure 2–1 illustrates the basic concept. Assume that a group of 200 men is chosen and the characteristic to be measured is height. The center of the bell curve represents the most frequently occurring heights, and the edges contain the heights that occur with diminishing frequency—in other words, the very tall and the very short. The diagram in Figure 2–1 shows a vertical line drawn through the mode (highest point, most frequently occurring event) of the bell curve and a zero is placed below the vertical line. Immediately to the left of the zero is a −1 and immediately to the right of the mode is 1. The area between the −1 and 1 represents the first standard deviation. Moving further to the left and right respectively are −2 and 2, which represent the second deviation of the bell curve. Moving even further out along the horizontal axis in either direction are −3 and 3, which represent the third standard deviation of the data being considered. (Without getting into the mathematics involved in the formula's makeup, the bell curve would include 68 percent of the 200 observations in the first standard deviation, an additional 29 percent in the second standard deviation, and approximately 3

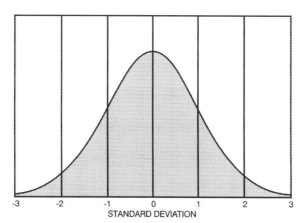

STANDARD DEVIATION

Figure 2–1   A normal distribution with the first 3 standard deviations in each direction indicated.

percent in the third standard deviation.) Please excuse the simplifications regarding the bell curve, but this is all that needs to be understood at this time.

I still remember the page of the textbook where it said that through the bell curve, out of apparent chaos comes a beautiful cosmic order. This hit home because I knew that my trading observations and experiences up to this time lacked a sense of order. I began trying to visualize the organization of the seemingly chaotic activity in the commodity pits—the chaos that everyone else accepted unquestioningly—within the structure of the bell curve. My job would be to find a way to bring order to that chaos, and the bell curve would be the tool.

At this point, the idea remained simply an image with no hard work or evidence to back it up. But it remained in the back of my mind for some time, waiting to be developed. My personal trading had moved from being based on wire house recommendations to newsletter recommendations. Although both good and bad recommendations were available, I fell into the habit of following the bad recommendations and being afraid to take the good ones. Soon I realized I could not just buy a trading program off the shelf or subscribe to a newsletter from a wire house. I had to create my own trading program.

After about a year and a half at Berkeley, I decided that I had learned all I could in college, yet I wanted my degree. I felt that I had a natural bent toward trading, but what I was learning in school would not be directly relevant to my career as a commodities trader. So after my sophomore year, I decided to give Berkeley 1 more year, and I doubled up on all my units so as to finish my program within that time.

During the summer of 1959, I took a finance course that introduced me to the principles of value investing through the classic work of Graham and Dodd. Their book, *Security Analysis,* made a lot of sense because I had already learned from observation and from talking with my father that in any market the relationship between price and value was the key—that price away from value usually represented opportunity. I made the immediate association of using the bell curve to find value in the marketplace, although I still did not see how I was going to do this. The idea of using the concepts of Graham and Dodd in conjunction with the bell curve clearly intrigued me. I felt that a merging of the bell curve with Graham and Dodd would provide a sound basis from which to approach the market. My goal became to find out how to merge them.

John Schultz and the Minimum Trend

Now I had entered a new phase of my trading career. I realized that I had to broaden my knowledge base if I hoped to be successful. So I went out and bought every book I could find about commodity trading, markets, stocks, and successful traders. I tried to glean from these books a program whereby I could see what was happening in the markets. I began to realize that, although the people I was reading about had different approaches and different styles, they must have been looking at the markets the same way because they were all unsuccessful. It is said that almost 90 percent of the people who trade commodities lose money. Commodity markets were not recommended for anybody. So what was the common thread running through the books? The diagrams were really beautiful, but they were all trying to predict the market.

That was the problem. Graham and Dodd had opened my eyes to value. They had explained that value could be seen in the present tense rather than on a predictive basis. One could understand the present by laying out all the conditions that currently prevailed and then noting the changes that took place. One of the best books I read at this time was a short dissertation called *A Treatise on Charting* by John Schultz. (It was self-published and is no longer available.) In reading this book, everything came together for me. I realized that there was a lot of potential in the marketplace and that I had to have a way of making decisions. I had to know what I was doing, why I was doing it, and under what conditions I was doing it. Then I would be able to see and interpret changes as they happened. That was the beginning of my formulation of a plan for trading.

The key idea on which I seized was Schultz's concept of the minimum trend. Schultz defined the minimum trend as the smallest unit of meaningful market activity. This does not mean focusing on each and every tick. It means the smallest unit of time and price activity that could develop into a vertical move. One would use these minimum trends to measure market activity and to see when a change in the market was beginning. The advantage of this concept was that the aggregation of these minimum trends would eventually indicate the beginning of a directional move. This is because the minimum trend is one-sided. It can only get bigger, never smaller. The simplicity of this attracted me. I decided to use a 3-minute price range as my version of the minimum trend.

The next step was realizing that a number of minimum trends could be grouped statistically to form a bell curve. I came up with the idea that the bell curve could be used to represent an arrangement of behavior around price. The first standard deviation—the middle of the bell curve, where the majority of activity takes place (68%) would represent value, whereas the second and third standard deviations would measure price away from value. Whenever the market moved away from value, I would take the opposite side of the trade. Please look at Figure 2–2 to the points

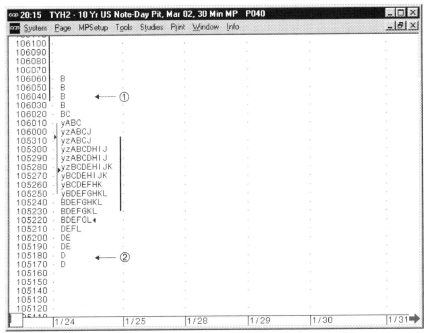

Figure 2–2   Minimum trends grouped statistically to form a bell curve.

illustrated. I would sell the zone indicated by the number 1 or buy the zone indicated by the number 2 because I felt that the market would return to value (the center of the bell curve).

Thus for the first time, I would have a reason for making trading decisions—a reference point for trading. And, although this idea wasn't fully developed at the time, I want to explain it further now because it proved to be so important.

Charting the Minimum Trend

The commodities markets were very different in the early 1960s than they are now. They moved very slowly, and it might take as much as a week or two to fill in the bell curve completing a small directional move or distribution, as they came to be known in Market Profile. An important distinction should be made between two types of markets—the initiative market and the responsive market. An initiative market is one characterized by buying as the price moves higher and away from value or selling as the price moves lower and away from value. This might occur, for example, if an earnings warning was issued by XYZ Corporation. Prices would move directionally lower (distributing) to find a new fair price. Initiating selling would enter the market in the belief that the directional move will continue.

Figures 2–3 and 2–4 are Market Profile graphics showing initiating activity. We know we are putting the cart in front of the horse by showing profile displays before explaining what a Market Profile is; however, in the context of what we are trying to do, we feel justified in doing so. To determine whether activity is initiating or responsive we need to use the previous day's value area as our reference. In the following four examples, we assume that the leftmost profile is the previous day's profile and the rightmost profile is the current day's profile. The dark solid vertical line to the right of the profile represents that day's value area. Figure 2–3 shows 2 days of profiles for American Airlines (AMR). Note that on 1/28 (date along bottom), the profile looks like a normal bell curve with the day's value referenced by the solid vertical line. The "previous day's" value area is the information we use to determine if activity is initiating or responsive. The following day (1/29), the letters (which represent half-hour trading periods) traded opposite value or below the value area of

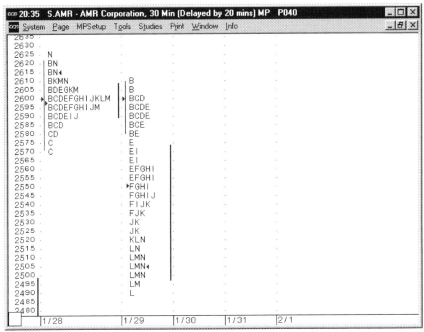

Figure 2–3   American Airlines with initiating selling.

1/28. Also note that for the profile dated 1/29, the letters chronologically (representing half-hour trading periods) had many instances throughout the day where they traded lower (E, F, J, K, and L), signaling selling. The day is a textbook example of initiating selling (selling below value).

Figure 2–4, Phelps Dodge Corporation (PD), shows initiating activity once again, but in this case initiating buying. Make note of the value area for the previous day (1/30), which is referenced with the dark solid vertical line to the right of the profile for the day. Then look at the current day's (1/31) price activity (half-hour ranges represented by chronological letters) and note that on many instances throughout the day the letters traded higher (C, E, F, I, and N), indicating buying. The buying above the previous day's value area is a textbook example of initiating buying.

In a responsive market, participants act just the opposite. As a market moves higher or lower (away from the previous day's value), sellers or buyers enter the market feeling that the market will not continue moving directionally. They feel it is just a matter of time before the market trades back to what is considered an area of established value. They respond to a directional move up by selling into it or a directional move down by buying it.

Figures 2–5 and 2–6 illustrate responsive buying and selling, respectively. Once again, the first step in assigning activity as initiating or responsive is to determine the previous day's value area. Looking at Figure 2–5, which is Ford Motor Company (F), one can locate the value area for 1/31, which is represented by the dark solid vertical line opposite the profile for that day. Note the price activity for the following day (2/1): the market opened lower (B, first half-hour of trade for stocks) and managed to trade higher (C). In other words, the lower open triggered buying by participants who saw these lower prices as being below value.

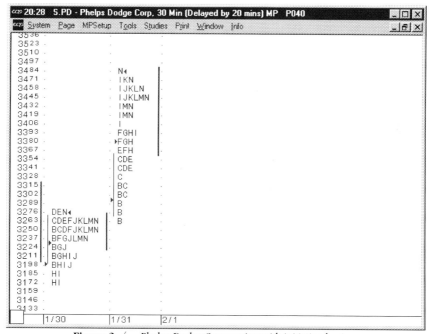

Figure 2–4   Phelps Dodge Corporation with initiating buying.

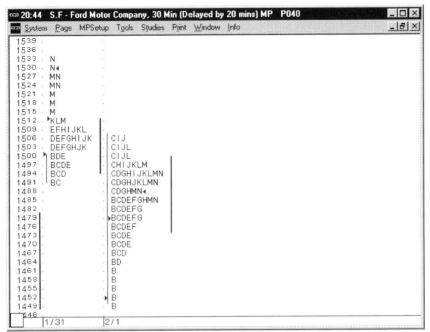

Figure 2–5   Ford Motor Company with responsive buying.

Figure 2–6 can be interpreted in the same fashion but from the opposite side of the ledger. Figure 2–6 is 2 days of profiles for Citigroup (C). Note the proximity of the value area for 1/23 and how the price activity unfolded on the following day (1/24). Knowing that individual stocks start trading in the "B" period, one can see that the market did open above the previous day's value. In fact, the first half of the day saw initiating buying (buying above the previous day's value) as C and G periods took out previous half-hour highs. Once the initiating buying reached a climax, sellers built up the courage to short the market. And sell it they did; one can see that H, I, J, M, and N periods saw rotations down versus previous half-hour's lows. In summary, Figure 2–6 had both initiating buying and responsive selling, with the selling winning out and driving prices back through most of the previous day's value area.

The 1960s were basically responsive markets and less volatile than the 1970s, which had much greater volatility and were characterized by more frequently occurring initiative activity. As one will see, the methods developed were especially well suited for responsive markets. What I worked out, without understanding it, was a way of charting trading volume. The underlying formula is simple:

Price + Time = Value

The 3-minute minimum trend chart I developed was really an indication of people using, or not using, various price areas of the market. These minimum trend units would form a bell curve looking something like Figure 2–7.

As you can see, Figure 2–7 is a perfect example of the so-called normal distribution of price/time usage in the market—a

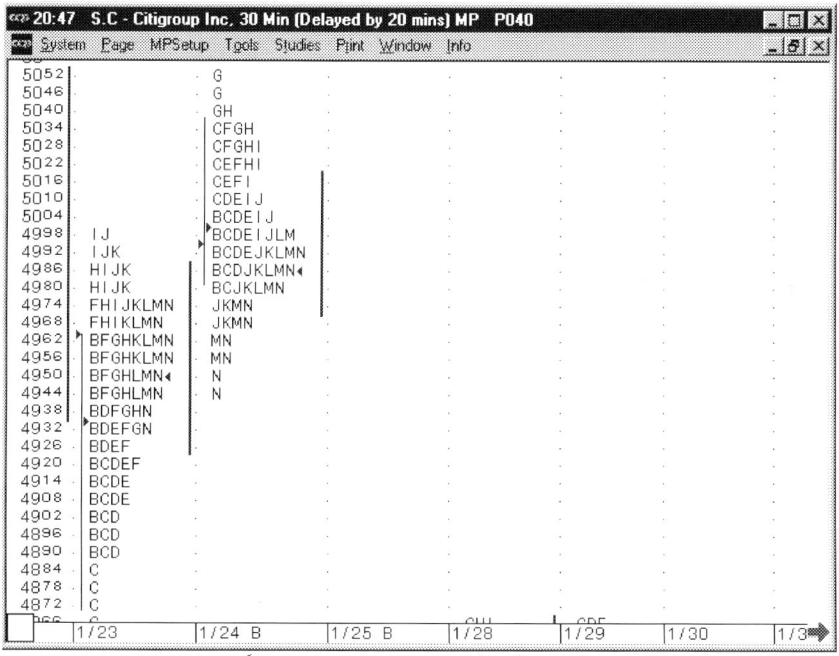

Figure 2–6 Citigroup Incorporated with responsive selling.

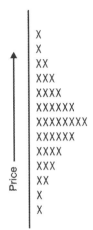

Figure 2–7   Drawn bell curve.

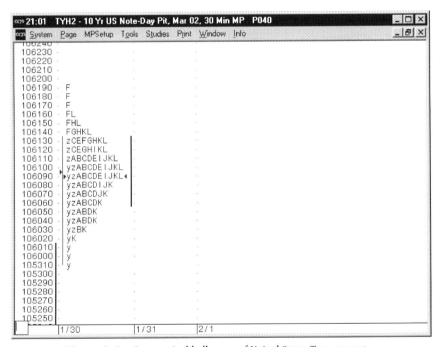

Figure 2–8   Symmetrical bell curve of United States Ten-year note.

perfect bell curve. This is the form responsive markets took, and still take today. If one looks at a profile of any responsive market of today, one will find a symmetrical pattern of much the same sort. Figure 2–8 is an example on a symmetrical bell curve in the March 10-year notes.

As a trader, I was basically playing for this symmetrical pattern to develop using the number of minimum trends at each price level as a timing device. I would play for the high-volume price to be at or close to the middle of the day's price range. A trader could fade or go against a higher or lower opening in any market, and this strategy would work about 95 percent of the time—again reflecting the responsive nature of the markets. My simple strategies worked well at the time—much better than the same strategies would work today. To illustrate my trading technique in the 1960s, assume we had a half-completed distribution at the end of a trading day. The minimum trend profile might look like Figure 2–9. The Xs represent the prices traded for the day. The following day, the market opened two ticks lower at 97 (assuming the previous day's close was 99). Under these conditions, I would be a buyer of the market knowing that the market was unbalanced and must come to balance in a responsive situation. I would be counting the number of minimum trends at each price (reflected by the number of Xs arranged horizontally at each price) and playing the fill-in, knowing that when the bell curve was completely filled in, I would be out of time at each price. Thus, I was using time rather than price as the key factor in my trading. Figure 2–10 shows the second day's activity, following that of Figure 2–9. The Os represent the minimum trends on Day 2.

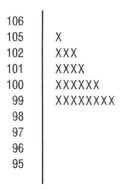

```
106 |
105 | X
102 | X X X
101 | X X X X
100 | X X X X X
 99 | X X X X X X X X
 98 |
 97 |
 96 |
 95 |
```

Figure 2–9 Hypothetical minimum trend profile.

```
105
104   │ X
103   │ XXX
102   │ XXXX
101   │ XXXXX
100   │ XXXXXXX
 99   │ OOOOOO
 98   │ OOOO
 97   │ OOO
 96   │ O
 95   │
```

Figure 2–10   Day 2 of hypothetical minimum trend profile.

By counting the minimum trend units and looking for the completion of the bell curve (in both Xs and Os), I could see when the market had become efficient and completed a distribution. The move was over. I had accomplished my first objective in trading by developing this method. I could now understand where price was and the conditions surrounding price.

I was thinking about the marketplace at the Chicago Board of Trade (CBOT) as a place to convert my ideas into opportunities—a forum for marketing my ideas. At the CBOT, I could market my ideas right in the pit. There would always be someone to take the opposite side of a transaction and the right thinking would win.

During 1960, I served in the U.S. Army and throughout my time in the service, I always had the commodity markets on my mind. I had previously wanted to do something in agriculture, but opportunities there seemed closed because it was a high-capital, low-margin game. By contrast, I felt I could trade with a low-capital, high-ability strategy. So the CBOT seemed like the place for me. Although I had the educational background, the ideas, and the desire to go forward, I still lacked the confidence, the courage, and the capital to get started.

I stumbled around for about 6 months after getting out of the service. My father would clip job ads from the paper for me and tell me that I should not be "too proud" to work for someone else. But I just kept on doing what I wanted to do—trying to put together real estate deals, trying different things. I was still sorting things out and looking for a direction in my life.

Chapter 3

CHICAGO

In January 1962, I decided to go to Chicago to see what was there. I did not know where I was going. I did not know where LaSalle Street was. I did not know where the Board of Trade building was. I did not know anybody in Chicago—but I was going.

False Start

I said goodbye to my parents and arrived in Chicago on a cold, miserable day in February. There was snow in the streets, and it was black with coal dust. It was not very appealing to a young man from California. I went straight to the Board of Trade and proceeded up to the balcony overlooking the trading floor. My hope for market liquidity disintegrated. Down below were a bunch of empty pits. There were about six people standing in the soybean pit, and there was no activity—no runners, no phones ringing, nothing going on. I decided to go back to California. When I got home, I worked on my brother-in-law's farm and helped my father around the ranch. But I spent most of my time dreaming up real estate deals, trying to put deals together, knocking on doors, and getting turned down. I thought my business ideas were sound, but people did not like them. I was constantly scheming up deals that would allow me to make money without money, but no one was willing to fill in the other side of the equation. Nevertheless, I was confident something was going to happen.

A good situation was developing in soybeans in the spring of 1963. A low carryover from the previous year and a dry planting season brought on a good price move up—about 30 cents a bushel. Although I had not yet developed a charting method, I was trading the minimum trend. I was just visualizing prices and using my mental images of the bell curve as a guide. I caught most of the up move in soybeans and got out near the high. When the market went back down, I repurchased soybeans and got out when they went back up again. I felt really good about this because it reinforced my idea of grouping prices and then trying to buy or sell prices outside of value. This little bit of experience gave me the confidence to go back to Chicago. I told a friend of mine, who was also my broker, what I was planning to do, and he decided to go out there with me. This was in the fall of 1963.

Breaking In

As I left for Chicago, I had all my money in the soybean market despite the fact that my father was advising me to "start fresh." I was long 100,000 bushels of soybeans with 17 cents profit. I was sure they would go up a dollar, and I would make $100,000. I wish I had listened to my father. I left for Chicago on Thursday, and by Friday soybeans were down the limit; they were supposed to be down another 7 cents on Monday. When I got out, all my profit and all my capital had vanished.

I was starting out in Chicago with no money, no friends, and not much to go on. I was staying at the Fort Dearborn Hotel for $1.50 a night. I would wake up crying in the morning, thinking about the great opportunity I had lost because of my mismanagement and impatience. I was able to borrow some money to buy my membership on the Chicago Board of Trade (CBOT) and the membership committee approved me on October 23, 1963. I was self-conscious about trading with open outcry, so I would just stand on the edge of the pit and keep track of minimum trends and groupings on paper. Everybody thought I was a conventional chartist. In fact, when I went to pay my membership fees, the secretary of the exchange said to me, "I understand you use those charts. We've had a lot of people come and go with those things." I turned to him and said, "Well, if you knew so much, you wouldn't be secretary of the exchange. You'd be down there trading." At first, he was taken aback by my brashness. But he respected my candor and eventually became a lifelong friend. My approach to trading remained the same. I had to have a reason to buy or sell, and I would be right or wrong based on that reason. If I was consistently wrong, I would have to do the opposite of what the indicator told me. Even with my relative lack of experience, I had confidence in my ability to read and understand the market.

One afternoon, I was invited out for lunch by two acquaintances, one a member of the CBOT board of directors and the other a member of the New York Stock Exchange. When we finished lunch, they asked me what I thought about the market. I told them I was taking very small positions because I wanted to "build my factory." In other words, I wanted to be able to make a series of small trades and come out with a profit. After building a base in this way, I would up my volume.

Both of the men with whom I was having lunch were experienced traders, and that day they had positions that were opposite to me at the end of the day. It troubled me that I might be doing something wrong because these men were obviously very successful. The next morning I considered getting out of my positions on the open, but I decided to give my trade a little time. Within a couple of hours, the market went my way. I knew then that although I did not have as much experience or direct knowledge as the other people in the market, I had a good sense of how the market was organized, and I was on the road to becoming a good trader.

I attribute my early success to the character of the market at the time. In the early 1960's, the market was both active and responsive, which allowed my basic game plan to work. I came in with a simple program of buying low and selling high. I figured that if I bought low and it stayed low, I would get out; and if I sold high and it stayed high, I would get out. The commodity markets were not very volatile back then. A soybean move of a dollar would be considered a really big move. Generally, everything moved 10 or 15 cents a bushel all year. Today, we get moves of that magnitude in 15 minutes.

Success in a Responsive Market

I was firmly convinced that I had the best idea out there. I was going to measure the market in terms of time, and I was going to measure market conditions in the present tense. In an uncertain market, it is hard to predict with better than a fifty-fifty shot. Rather than predicting, the idea is to try to understand current market conditions. As Graham and Dodd had shown, the value of a stock is determined by underlying conditions. If conditions change, value changes.

I found it very useful to spend my afternoons studying my purchase and sale sheet from the previous day to see whether I had been reacting properly or failing to take advantage of the full potential of my trades. I used this as an opportunity for critical self-analysis. I might say, "I bought soybeans right at the low to-day, but I took only a quarter of a cent profit. What did I do wrong?" This practice of self-analysis became a key element in what I called my equation for success:

$$\text{Market Understanding} \times \text{You} = \text{Results}$$

In my first year of trading, I found out several key things that played a major role in the development of my theory of markets. I did this without any research. It came from experience and observation. While gaining trading experience, I was also learning how markets work and how to read them. One belief I have always had is that young people adapt to situations very well. Like seeds in a greenhouse, they grow to fit their environment. When stress comes—when the temperature changes within the greenhouse or the roof falls in—they have to make an adjustment. Seven or 8 years usually pass before that happens to a young trader just coming on the floor. I was lucky to start out in a responsive market with a responsive trading program. I do not know whether I would have survived in an initiating-style trading market.

When I first came to Chicago, we had very few initiating days, but when they did occur I always lost money. I could see this because my minimum trends showed an imbalance. I would get hurt on such days because I did not anticipate when the market was going to change. My basic style was not to go with the market, but to go against it. I knew how to trade a responsive market, but not an initiating-type market.

Learning by Observation

Because I did not know anybody in the pit, I was not distracted by conversations with friends. I developed the habit of observing closely the people around me. I was always trading well when the pit was full of people. This was because when the pit was full, the market was apt to continue moving in the same direction. When the pit emptied out, it was a period of low activity, meaning that the market would change direction. Often, I would still have my position on, and when the pit filled up again the market would often go in the opposite direction. This happened to me enough times during my first 2 months in Chicago that I began to get out of my position when I saw the market stop and the pit empty out. Then when the pit filled up again, I would go with the new market direction. Later, when I formalized my understanding of the markets, I realized that this was related to the phenomenon of trade facilitation. When the market stops trading actively, it is near the end of the directional move.

Exposure, Excesses, and the Long- and Short-Term Trader

There were a lot of successful traders on the floor who had name recognition and followings of their own. Whenever one of them traded, a lot of other traders would come in behind them and ride their coattails. The good traders took advantage of this. They knew that there was going to be a lot of buying or selling behind them. The good trader would assess that buying or selling activity to see whether it pushed the market further. If it did not, he would be the first to get out. This "free peek" at the market was very important and a good advantage for the prominent traders. I realized that one key to trading success was exposure in the market place; and for the first time, I saw that market activity could be described by volume. The important thing to note was the amount of directional price move this caused.

I also noticed that on the days when the market changed, I usually lost money. When the market moved in one direction with a lot of volume, as a local trader, I would fade it and get hurt. Those 1 and 2 days a month, I was playing for the same norm that occurred on the other 18 trading days, and it was very difficult for me to make money. Because each bad day subtracted from my winning days, I figured that if I could recognize this type of day and refrain from trading, I would be money ahead. But what was most frustrating was that these losing days were the really active days in the market. In trying to classify trading days, I first discovered that we had two types of days. The first type was active early and ran out of gas during the day (responsive days). The second type comprised big days that developed all day (initiative days). Another observation I made—perhaps the

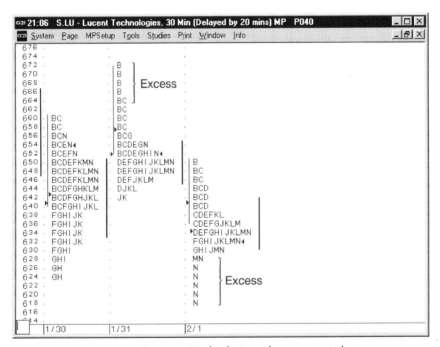

Figure 3–1   Lucent Technologies with excesses noted.

most important—had to do with the speed of price change. The faster the market moved away from a price, the more it indicated that the price was an excess or a noncompetitive area of the market. As a local trader, one learned to perceive this in varying degrees. The principle behind it was that this excessive price area—too high or too low—would act as a barrier against further price movement in that direction. This is one of the best reference points a trader can have. Fortunately or unfortunately, these excesses occur in varying sample sizes. But they are always there, and they can occur at any time during a trading session. It is extremely important to pick up on them to avoid a no-win situation. Figure 3–1 is a daily Market Profile of Lucent Technologies with the excess areas noted. If it is difficult to understand how this chart is configured, please see Chapter 6, where it is explained in great detail.

The Common Laws of the Market Place

Through my early trading experiences and observations, I began to see that all markets were basically the same. The commodity markets were no different from my father selling grain for a fair price or our ranch hands buying used cars or guns when the prices were attractive. The day trader and the investor are looking at the same price. The difference is that they are viewing it from different viewpoints. An example illustrates this point.

In the day area, the purpose of the market is to find a fair price so that trade can take place. (No one will intentionally trade at an unfair price.) In the beyond-the-day area, price regulates the activity of the long-term buyer or seller by moving up and down. For example, if there is a lot of building activity in a local real estate market, prices for labor and materials, interest rates, and other expenses will tend to hold or increase. A professional builder, being aware of market conditions, would be willing to pay currently high prices knowing that they are probably bargains compared with the prices coming in the near future. The builder's willingness to "pay up" would be indicative of a perception of longer-term value being present in the current market prices. This value would not be apparent to a nonprofessional. If in the following year, the building activity is cut in half (owing to decreased demand), prices builders are willing to pay for labor, materials, and like expenses will probably fall—the old supply-demand equation. The combination of short-term and long-term activity creates an opportunity for those who discern it.

Observations like these give a set of circumstances that can be dealt with logically as traders. By following my experiences and observations during my early years in Chicago, the reader is probably beginning to see that it is possible to read the market in the present tense, not just after the fact. Learning to do this is a definite advantage for a trader.

Chapter 4

CHANGING MARKETS

After about 5 years of trading at the Chicago Board of Trade (CBOT), I began to see the need for some changes in my trading methods. What does one do when the indicators one is accustomed to leaning on no longer work? Experience is the best form of knowledge; but occasionally one comes to a point at which experience must be chucked and new insights gained. This is especially true in a dynamic, changing market place. In such a market, change equals opportunity. For example, one day, early in my trading years, I was an active corn buyer at the opening. A very nice old gentleman with about 30 years' trading experience tapped me on the shoulder and said, "Son, do you see those rail car loadings in Chicago? That means the commercial people are going to be sellers. I advise you to get out of the market." I thanked the old gentleman for his opinion—he was trying to help a young trader out—but I disregarded his advice. I knew that the rail car theory was outdated and no longer reflected the market.

The Advent of Commodity Trading Funds

The first major change I had to adjust to when trading on the floor of the CBOT occurred in the late 1960s. For the first time, we had trading by commodity mutual funds that would buy huge quantities at higher than high prices. Prices would go up, and instead of selling, the funds would buy. This was the beginning of the historic change in the percentage of responsive to initiating activity. The activity of these commodity funds made me realize that enough money could drive the market far enough against me that my position would become so unfavorable in terms of risk versus reward that I would be continually forced to exit my positions. This was hard for me to deal with because I had always felt that no one could hurt me unless I was wrong. That was no longer the case. Now my capital was more at risk than ever before.

During the 1968–69 period, more and more commodity trading funds came into being. The floor trader's strategy was to let the funds push the price way out of line and then try to guess when they would end their activity. The idea was not to be the first to buy or sell to the funds, but to try to make the last trade. Hopefully, the funds would have moved the market to an extreme and if one were the last to sell or buy, one could wait for the smoke to clear and prices would begin to revert to the mean (responsive activity moving price back to the center of the bell curve). However, the volume of trading generated by the funds created a problem for the floor traders in that there was usually a large distribution (directional price move) with accompanying volume. This meant that the market would continue moving directionally (initiative activity), taking away any advantage from making the last trade as well. A contemporary example of this type of activity from a macro perspective was the Internet Initial Public Offering (IPO) bubble of 1999 and 2000. No matter how high the prices ran initially, one could not afford to sell. Each price rise was greeted with a new wave of initiative activity that would propel prices dramatically higher. The Internet bubble was the antithesis of the grain markets of the 1960s. The one time it was safe to sell into initiative activity was when the funds drove the price high enough to give us an excess—a quick fall away from the price peak.

These excesses in price coincided with a newfound volatility in the market. My confidence level declined at this time because I really did not know how to handle this activity. I was smart enough not to take any chances by selling into ridiculous prices because things were changing. I had to reassess my position and my approach to the market.

My earlier approach had worked for some time, but it was no longer viable because the potential profits were small in relation to the moves that were taking place. I realized this and my volume of trading declined not because of losses, but because I needed to figure out a new approach. I needed to fix the broken gate rather than ignore it.

I have always found it important to be in control of myself and hopefully of the market. The importance of this had been brought home to me when I was first starting in Chicago. I was long 25 soybeans, and the market was up 6 cents. This meant $1,500 profit for the day—a tremendous amount of money for me at the time—but I knew the position was worth a lot more than that. So I decided to ride it out even though the market might set back. At first, it did set back to the point where my $1,500 profit had declined to an $800 profit. But it moved sharply my way several days later, and I ended up making a larger profit on the trade. I won because I was in control of the market and my emotions at all times. My decision was based not on money but on opportunity.

Now, several years later, the market had changed. It seemed that I could no longer control the situation as I had with the 25 beans back in 1965. So I was trying to buy rallies and sell breaks a little more often. This was extremely difficult to do because I had begun my career as a responsive trader. Now my trading style had to adjust to the market to survive. I could understand the need for the market to change to attract new participants and grow, but I was not adapting to the change. I was avoiding the situation. It took me about 6 months to regain control. Once I did, I could buy rallies or sell breaks without being nervous. I was back in step with the markets. This reinforces the meaning of my basic equation for success:

$$\text{Market Understanding} \times \text{You} = \text{Results}$$

The 1970s proved to be an exciting decade for commodities owing to the tremendous upheavals in most sectors of our economy. But it would have been a traumatic period for me had I not been able to make the earlier adjustment. Many people who were successful during the 1970s lost their money in the 1980s because the markets changed again, but they did not. I had a friend on the floor who had amassed a small fortune only to lose it in 6 months because he never modified his program. One of the keys to being a successful trader over a period of time is to adapt to change. You must be able to find a new program when the old one is not working, and have the discipline to implement it.

The 1970s: Greater Markets, Greater Opportunities

All this time, I was using the same minimum trend charting format, but the markets were getting broader and broader, and there was a lot more opportunity. It got to the point where I could not keep my minimum trend notations on the piece of paper I was carrying, so I began doing it mentally. I would visualize where the range of the first standard deviation (the value area) was taking place, and then I would mentally plot the prices above and below this area. Refer to Figure 4–1, the bell curve.

My strategy had become mainly one of follow through. The new strategy was to be an initiative-type trader. Instead of selling when the market left the first standard deviation (the value area) on the upside, as a responsive trader would do, I would initiate a trade going with the direction of the market away from the first standard deviation. I would look to see if the move generated increased volume. If it did not show increasing volume, I would begin to get out of the position. The significance of vol-

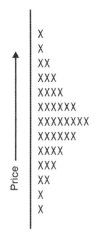

Figure 4–1   Bell curve.

ume refers back to a lesson mentioned earlier. If higher prices did not bring in additional volume then the higher prices were not facilitating trade (creating interest) and the higher price would be moved away from. Just like when the pit was full, it would mean that the market was apt to continue moving directionally because the price activity was generating interest. Conversely, when the pit emptied, it indicated a lack of interest (volume) that would likely lead to a reversal of direction or rejection.

My strategy had changed. Now it was unusual for me to get in front of the market in a responsive way as I had in the 1960s. I was mainly following the first standard deviation, then going with the market direction when it left the first standard deviation. The markets were so dynamic in those days that even a small move was more than enough of a range from which to operate.

Another change that occurred in the 1970s was in the speed of decisions required by the trader. Generally speaking, a responsive trade is a trade for tomorrow in that one is fading the near-term price activity and the market needs to stop and eventually go the other way. One had almost all day to make the trade because the markets were simply not very volatile. Initiating trades call for an immediate response because there is a tendency for the trade to get away from one before one can act.

Narrow-Range Days and New Activity

There were not many slow markets in the 1970s, but whenever they did occur I wondered how I could possibly make a living in this business. I traded hard but it was almost impossible to make money. No orders were coming in and there was no range. There was no way I could force the market to make money for me. The day after one of these slow sessions, I would get in there and take a position. I would buy 10 contracts of soybeans and the market would move up. I would take a cent profit and have a $500 return—and I was glad to get it. I took the sure thing every time. But 9 times out of 10, it would turn out to be a real big day, where the 10 contracts would turn out to be worth $10,000 instead of $500. After a slow day, one doesn't see a lot of opportunity in the market, so one is inclined to be cautious and conservative. This is often the wrong time to play it safe because these narrow-range days were often the setup for a new directional move. One had to see them as an opportunity. One day the market would not be doing anything and the next day would be a big one. These narrow-range days often marked the end of one trend and the setup for a new trend.

Chapter 5

THE INFORMATION REVOLUTION

In the early 1980s, the Chicago Board of Trade (CBOT) sparked an information revolution by making available information that had never before been disseminated by the market place. The effect of this revolution was to demystify the markets by allowing people on the outside to easily determine what everyday traders were doing. The cloak of secrecy had been removed from the exchange and its participants, allowing the public access to the "underground" world of trading.

Opening Up the Market

When I was elected a director of the CBOT in 1981, I was given responsibility for market information. From my base at the statistical department, I felt that by bringing a lot more information out to the public, we could change the closed image of the industry into a more open one. At that time, Les Rosenthal, the chairman of the exchange, was a strong supporter of opening up the industry. In the early stages, our requests for information were pretty rudimentary. We just wanted information on cleared trades from the clearinghouse. No one else had ever had these data. When our request came to Chairman Rosenthal's attention, he backed us. He understood that the CBOT would benefit from opening up. Without Mr. Rosenthal's strong support, the committee would not have had the information needed to formalize data from the markets nor the money required to carry out this important work.

The only real project criterion that Chairman Rosenthal gave me was not to do anything that could harm the markets of the CBOT. I shared this concern. My friends' memberships were worth a lot. I did not want to be part of something that could jeopardize their livelihoods.

The anxiety about what our work might mean spread through the industry. Rumors were everywhere. One story had it that local traders would no longer be needed, and that they were already being eliminated in Bermuda and at other exchanges. Some said Chicago would be next.

Of course, the information revolution did not harm the markets or the local traders. It benefited them greatly. But at the time, what we were trying to do was so new that many people did not understand it.

Price Recurrence and Volume

The information revolution of the early 1980s provided price data but never in a manner that would show how the market was behaving. Was it being responsive? Did the market activity indicate initiative activity? As is discussed later in the book, this new charting system has a value-added aspect. It not only shows prices occurring at specific times but also visually communicates the type of market activity that these prices reflect. That was the goal—a charting system that communicated both price and market condition.

The Natural Organization of the Market—Revealed

As we ran our initial market information programs at the CBOT in 1981, we saw that all the commodities we plugged into them revealed a beautiful sense of cosmic order, just as it said in my 1958 statistics textbook. The classic shape of the bell curve appeared on our screen (see Fig. 5–1).

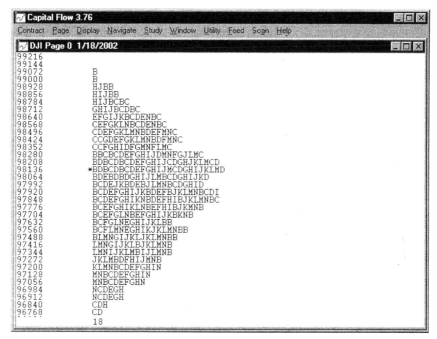

Figure 5–1 Bell curve.

The first standard deviation using 68 percent of volume on a normal day was right in the middle of the price/time relationship (Price + Time = Value). Our data and program had captured the market's natural organization. The public speculator now had a charting system that allowed him to relate to the basic market equation: (Price + Time = Value). People could now associate a certain price over a period of time with value. The off-the-floor trader could now get the same visual imprint of the market that I received while standing in the pit during the day.

It was difficult trying to fulfill a new role in the marketplace—that of providing real-time information. The CBOT deserves a lot of credit for its leadership in initiating the project. Between 1981 and 1984, we worked long and hard on it and spent lots of money. Now that work was coming to fruition for the good of the entire industry. I think a lesson has emerged that all exchanges must heed. The exchanges are information centers. The more information they disseminate, the more people will trade and the more successful the exchanges will be.

Fundamental and Technical Information

Because we have been discussing the importance of information in the marketplace, let us take a moment to consider the various sources of information available to a trader and how they should be used. Two main types of information need to be applied in the market place—fundamental and technical.

Fundamental information allows one to build a background and to place price in perspective. These are probably the two most important disciplines for a trader to develop. They allow one to take advantage of situations and enable one to sense opportunities. They make it possible to trade with confidence as one learns to "feel" the market. Fundamental information is constantly available: from the news, trade journals, government offices, corporate news releases, and so on. However, it is hard to acquire and use fundamental information in a timely fashion early in a trading career because one cannot yet relate it to the actual trading process. One must build a bank of actual trading experience which the fundamental information can be related to, and this takes time. The difficulty in using fundamental information is that one must interpret the data. Then this interpretation must be overlaid on the market itself. This calls for timing.

Sometimes one has the "right" data, only to discover that the market is doing something else. Most fundamental information should be used only as background. It can serve as a direct guide for trading only when price is very advantageous in relation to the data, or when the market is acting in accordance with the data. The difficulty of getting information on time and then applying it correctly has made fundamental information very hard to work with. As a result, most people do not use it.

Conversely, technical information comes in a nice neat package. It appears to be so easy to use that people flock to it. Technical data can be easy to see and easy to apply—but good results are not so easy to achieve. The problem is that some technical data are good and some are bad; the trader must make choices, interpret, and then time the trade. Most traders make the mistake of using technical data as the basis for the decision-making process when in fact they should be used mainly for timing an idea. Technical data are usually based on the forward projection of past data. But making accurate forward projections is most difficult in any profession. Those who have mastered some technical skills can use them fairly well. Market Profile is technical information, but it is drawn from a different database than other forms of technical information. The Market Profile database is evolving real time and reflects only what is happening on the trading floor. Market Profile tries to identify the underlying conditions of the current market movement. Not only does Market Profile communicate current price activity, it also communicates whether market activity is likely to continue or change. This is done by the way Market Profile captures the development of trading activity by fully utilizing the horizontal dimension. This is the subject of the next chapter. All the parameters and definitions I prepared for Market Profile are sound because they are derived from my floor experience and represent the principal working parts of the market. Hopefully the reader will come to see that it communicates more information regarding market condition than other forms of charting.

Section II

The Hawkins Interpretation

Chapter 6

UNDERSTANDING MARKET PROFILE

Market Profile is different from previously existing charting techniques. It is the result of an effort to meld the concept of value investing as expressed by Graham and Dodd, the bell curve from statistics, and the work of John Schultz's minimum trend. This chapter presents a few of the basic terms and shows how the Market Profile is graphed. How to use Market Profile for trading stocks, stock indexes, and other futures contracts is also discussed.

The easiest way to explain a Market Profile chart is to display it with each time period in a separate column—what is seen with a standard 30-minute bar chart. Prices are in ascending order on the vertical axis. Figure 6–1 is a standard 30-minute bar chart of the Dow futures contract traded on the Chicago Board of Trade (CBOT). The bar on the left side of the screen has a range of 9884 to 9920 and represents trades occurring between 7:20 and 7:50 A.M. CST. Each successive bar to the right represents a chronological half-hour period of the day.

Figure 6–2 shows the Dow futures contract for February 1, 2002. It shows the same information as in Figure 6–1 but the half-hour ranges are displayed with letters instead of a vertical line. This is a Market Profile display split into 30-minute segments, not a customary practice; it is done in this example only to simplify its explanation. It is scaled in four-point intervals for illustrative purposes. The "y" period has 10 time/price opportunities (TPOs). A TPO is a price that the market took an opportunity to trade at during a specific 30-minute period. In this exam-

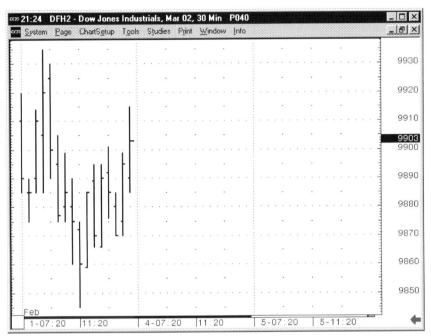

Figure 6–1   Standard 30-minute chart of the Dow futures contract.
Provided by CQG.

ple, "z" period has 5 TPOs and "A" period has 8 TPOs. If that were all there was to Market Profile it would be the same as a 30-minute bar chart.

Figure 6–3 has the same data as Figure 6–2; the only difference is that it has been graphed according to standard Market Profile criteria. Note that during "z" period if a price from "y" period is repeated, the chart expands horizontally by moving to the right one column (the same as a standard 30-minute bar chart). However, moving beyond the low tick of "y" period, the chart expands vertically, NOT horizontally. The z's between 9880 and 9872 are the first letters or TPOs at that price on that day so they go in the left-most column below the letter y.

Notice that the first time any price trades during the day, it automatically is placed in the left-most column. When the same price trades during a different time period later in the day, the recurring prices will move one column to the right. In Figure 6–3, the price of 9884 repeated in almost every half-hour segment of the day. The price of 9920 traded in only three half-hour periods (y, B, and C). In general, prices visited many times during the day will have a high number of TPOs, prices visited infrequently during the day will have few TPOs. If the day is highly directional, the profile will be more vertical and less horizontal. When a day has a lot of recurring prices, the Market Profile graphic will be more horizontal and less vertical.

Figure 6–4 of the Japanese yen illustrates this concept very succinctly. On January 30, the Market Profile graphic is very horizontal (more normalized) because the prices had a high degree of recurrence. On January 31, the Market Profile display is elongated (more vertical), with single prints throughout.

This use of the horizontal is the biggest difference between Market Profile and the conventional bar graph. In conventional charting, the horizontal is fixed because it automatically moves

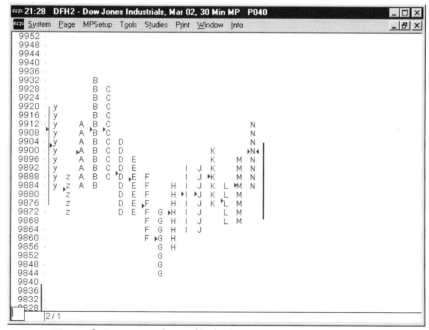

Figure 6–2 Dow Market Profile display split into 30-minute segments.

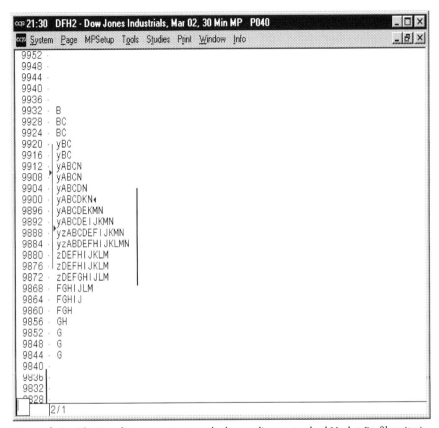

Figure 6–3   The Dow futures contract graphed according to standard Market Profile criteria. Copyright © 1984 Chicago Board of Trade. All Rights Reserved. CBOT Market Profile, Liquidity Data Bank, and LDB are registered trademarks of the Chicago Board of Trade. All Rights Reserved. Provided by CQG.

to the right at a defined time interval (30-minute, hourly, daily). This is not bad, but it is a limiting factor because there is no variance allowed in the display. Market Profile moves to the right only when a price repeats itself in a later period. Further examples will show that this allows Market Profile flexibility in the horizontal dimension.

Look again at Figure 6–2, the Market Profile display of the Dow futures contract. In z period, there are two outcomes. If a price repeats in z period that traded in y period, it moves to the right. When a new price is traded for the day (market expands vertically), it moves to the left-most column below the y. If the theory behind this charting technique is difficult to understand, create a chart by hand for theoretical stock XYZ. Have it trade as many TPOs as wanted during the first period. Stocks start trading at 8:30 A.M. CST; therefore the first half-hour of trade is assigned the letter B. At 9:00 A.M., the next time period (C) begins. Are the trade prices in C period a repeat of prices traded in B period? If the answer is yes, the chart will automatically expand horizontally. Move one column to the right and display the representative letter in that column. If the answer is no (because the trade price is higher or lower than the B period range), then the chart expands vertically. The TPO letters are placed above or below the first half-hour's range in the first column of the Market Profile graphic. That is how the Market Profile display formula works.

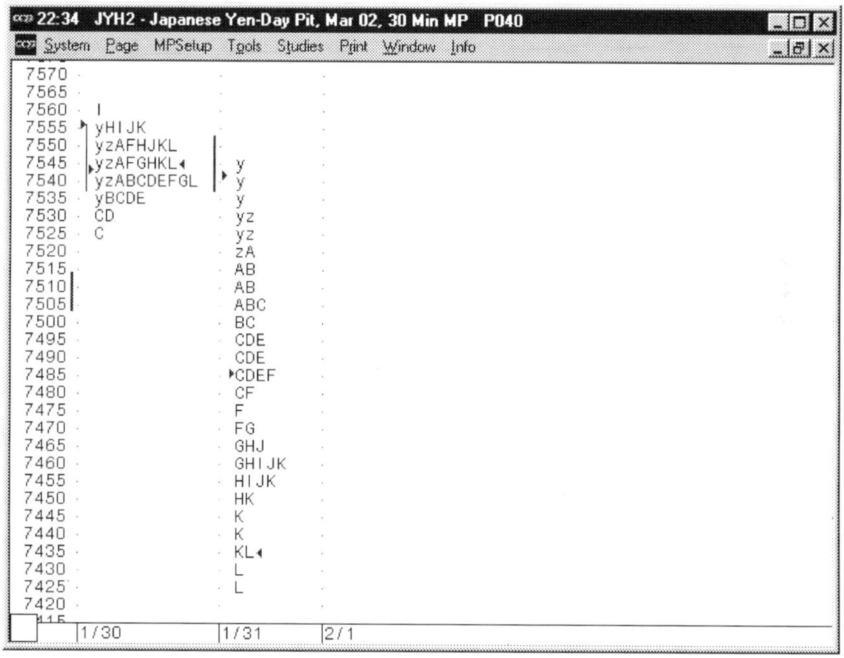

Figure 6–4   Japanese yen.

This is a somewhat philosophical point but it needs to be mentioned. Why is it that someone looks at a chart in the first place? They look at a chart to understand what is happening with a specific stock or commodity. The chart is a communication vehicle. Its purpose is to communicate current market conditions. The best charting system is the one that communicates the most information to the reader. A charting system that can express itself two ways in the horizontal dimension has an inherent advantage over a system that moves automatically to the right each half-hour. The rest of the book explains how to read all the information that Market Profile communicates.

Market Profile crystallized the basic trading concepts Mr. Steidlmayer acquired after 25 years on the floor. These included his understanding of how the market worked, along with various trading assumptions and disciplines that have proved effective and stood the test of time.

Basic Principles of Market Profile

Let us start by laying out three operating principles that are behind Market Profile. First, Market Profile is a form of technical analysis, in that the information derived from it is mechanical in nature; it comes from strict and objective parameters and definitions. The difference between ordinary technical analysis and Market Profile is that Market Profile uses the evolving market rather than past market history as its database.

Second, Market Profile is more of a present-tense, internal information source as opposed to other technical tools like moving averages and relative strength, which are external to the market. Market Profile attempts to replicate what a trader standing in the pit sees that allows market activity to be read as it develops.

A third difference between traditional technical analysis and Market Profile is that traditional technical analysis tries to predict the future based on the past. Market Profile tries to identify the underlying conditions of the current markets movement for continuation or change. These underlying conditions are expressed as the Market Profile expands horizontally, vertically, or in both directions. All of the parameters and definitions Mr. Steidlmayer prepared for Market Profile are sound because they are derived from experience and represent the principal working parts of the market. However, markets are dynamic and changing, and as they change new parameters and definitions are needed to represent the new areas of the market and the changes that have occurred.

The most noteworthy change taking place in the trading community today is electronic access. It has further globalized the industry and decreased the cost of doing business for most participants. Being a professional trader no longer requires spending hundreds of thousands of dollars on a membership at a stock or futures exchange. One needs only connectivity with an order-routing system. This allows for the most significant advantage of trading off the floor—mobility. By loading the order-routing system onto a computer, one is able to trade from home, office, while vacationing or commuting utilizing wireless technology.

Reading the Market Profile Chart

My intention is not to bore you with the details of how a Market Profile is created; however, it is the foundation on which our methodology is built. In the Market Profile chart, prices are arranged along the vertical axis (y axis), the highest price at the top and the lowest price at the bottom. Trading activity at each price is then graphically displayed on this chart. In the standard display, the trading day is divided into half-hour periods—a convenient, though arbitrary choice; some other time period could have been selected (some vendors allow for profiles to be displayed in user-defined segments, e.g., 5-minute, hourly, daily). These periods are labeled with a letter for the first period of the day, and then progressing alphabetically. When a trade occurs at a particular price during a particular half-hour segment, the letter for that period is displayed at the appropriate price point on the chart. As the day progresses, and trades occur at various prices during different half-hour periods, a unique Market Profile for that day and that product is developed using the bell curve.

The Market Profile presents a number of basic elements of the market in a rapidly understood graphic form. The smallest possible unit is the TPO—a single letter representing a trade occurring at a given price at a given time. This is a direct descendent of John Schultz's minimum trend concept (the starting point for Mr. Steidlmayer's thinking about markets).

A large horizontal bulge represents prices that occur often during the day, usually with the greatest volume of trade. The thinner parts of the profile represent prices that occur less often. In most cases, the middle of the profile represents the area of fair price, where most of the trading occurs; the top and bottom represent relatively unfair prices, highs and lows, respectively. By noting how widely dispersed the high and low price excesses are and how far they are from the fair-price area, we can also see the relative unfairness of the day's high and low prices, presenting some degree of imbalance.

In most cases, the Market Profile resembles a normal distribution curve, which, as statisticians have found, is the most common organizing principle in nature. Because market behavior is human behavior, it is logical to expect that prices would follow the same statistical patterns that govern other human groups.

The normal distribution form of the Market Profile also reflects the market phenomenon by which participation drops off as prices move higher or lower. Just as individual bidders in an auction market drop out as price increases, so the Market Profile curve tails off at the upper end of the price range; at the lower end, the curve tails off as sellers drop out of the market. This represents the declining volume of trade at these extreme price levels.

Another way of looking at the normal distribution presented in a Market Profile is through the concept of the standard deviation, also drawn from the science of statistics. The standard deviation is a way of measuring how far the values in any group of numbers vary from the mean, or average value in the group. In any normal distribution, values within a given number of standard deviations from the mean will occur with a predictable frequency. Normally, about two-thirds of the values will fall within 1 standard deviation from the mean; 95 percent of the values will fall within 2 standard deviations of the mean, and approximately 99 percent of the data will fall within 3 standard deviations of the mean. Figure 6–5 is a graphic representation of

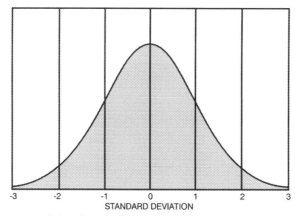

Figure 6–5 A normal distribution with the first 3 standard deviations in each direction indicated.

this. If the diagram is rotated 90 degrees clockwise, the Market Profile display appears.

Now that the reader understands what a Market Profile reveals, how can this information be used in analyzing market activity? Let us look at some details of how Market Profile reflects the development of a market as it happens.

The skill of reading Market Profile can be broken into two parts. The first deals with the individual day, the second with combining days. The interaction of these two "time frames" creates the conditions of opportunity. They need to be examined separately and then together to develop a good working understanding of Market Profile.

Day Structures: Five Typical Patterns

The purpose of the day structure is to find and maintain a fair price. This allows the market to do business because no one will intentionally trade at a price known to be unfair. This activity of the market in seeking and maintaining a fair price needs to be explained in relation to the day structure.

Study of the day structure begins with the first hour's price range—the range represented by the first two half-hour segments. This is defined as the initial balance area of the day. The accumulated trades in this area represent a beginning fair price for specialists and locals, for they account for a large amount of the trade during the first hour.

This is all well and good for them, but other traders soon come in to take advantage of price. These are generally beyond-the-day traders. Their activity upsets the delicate balance and price has to move to make an adjustment. If they give the market only a little nudge, price will not move very far; if they give it a big push, price will move rather dramatically.

By using the initial balance (first hour's trade) as a base, it is possible to project daily ranges based on the measured activity of outside longer-term participants (beyond-the-day trader). The beyond-the-day trader activity can range from extremely low to extremely high. This activity leaves a "footprint" in the market, which we have quantified and categorized as the five types of day structure.

First, there is the nontrend day. On a nontrend day, long-term traders exert little or no influence on the market. The market exhibits no or almost no extension of its range of prices beyond what is seen in the first hour. Additionally, the day's range is usually small. The Market Profile for January 28 in Figure 6–6 is a good example of a nontrend day. The first hour's prices are represented by the C and D prints in the profile; note that the range for the day was not extended beyond the first hour's range—a nontrend day. The reason the day unfolds into a nontrend-type day is because beyond-the-day traders see little opportunity/advantage to trading existing prices.

The next possibility is a day in which the market gets a slight push from the beyond-the-day traders, usually resulting in a slight extension beyond the initial balance. We call this a normal day. On a normal day, outside or long-term activity represents about 10 to 20 percent of the trading activity for the day and it produces a directionally biased range extension of about 50 percent beyond the first hour's range. In Figure 6–7 the profile dated January 30 would be categorized as a normal day. The first hour's range (y and z) was 12 ticks and the expansion beyond that range was 6 ticks. Typically on either a normal day or a nontrend day, the first standard deviation will be in the

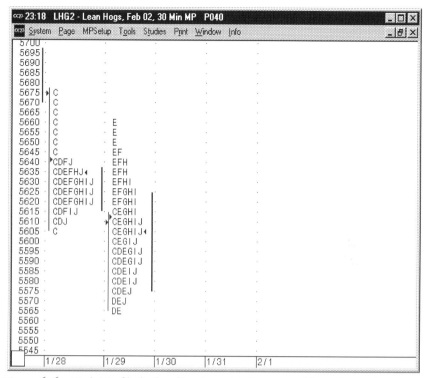

Figure 6–6 Market Profile display of lean hogs showing nontrend day and normal variation day on January 28 and January 29 respectively.

Copyright © 1984 Chicago Board of Trade. CBOT Market Profile, Market Profile, Liquidity Data Bank, and LDB are registered trademarks of the Chicago Board of Trade. All Rights Reserved. Provided by CQG.

middle of the range with the second and third standard deviations above and below.

The next type of day we call a normal variation day. It takes place when the longer-term trader represents 20 to 40 percent of the activity for the day. As a rule, on a normal variation day, the day's expansion is about double the range of the first hour's trade. In Figure 6–6 the profile display for January 29 is a good example of a normal variation day. On this day, the first hour's trading range was 11 ticks (C and D periods). Later in the day, longer-term traders came in and expanded the range higher by some 9 ticks, which satisfies our criterion of doubling the first hour's range.

Moving out on the curve, the next type of day is the trend day. On a trend day, the outside traders represent about 40 to 60 percent on the market's activity. The market moves dramatically away from its opening price range. It normally closes within 10 percent of the extreme in the direction of its movement during the day. Additionally, the first hour's range is typically small. Also note that half-hour ranges are directional. By that I mean the day should hold directional integrity with successive higher half-hour highs and higher half-hour lows or lower highs and lower lows. On this day, the buyers or sellers have used up all their bullets so the next day is not a good envi-

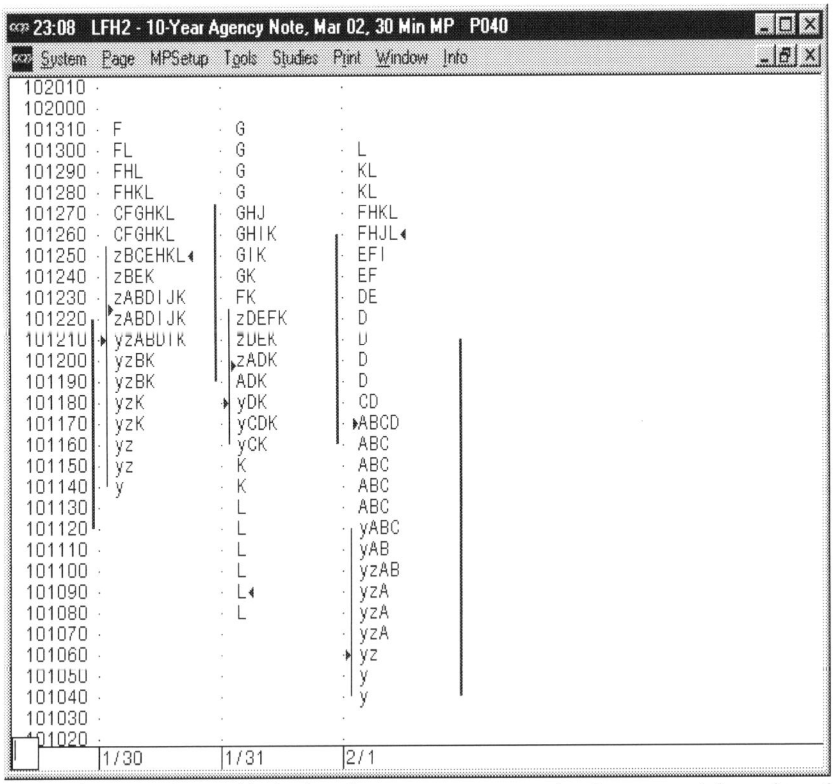

Figure 6–7   Market Profile display of 10-year agency notes showing a normal day and trend day on January 30 and February 1 respectively.

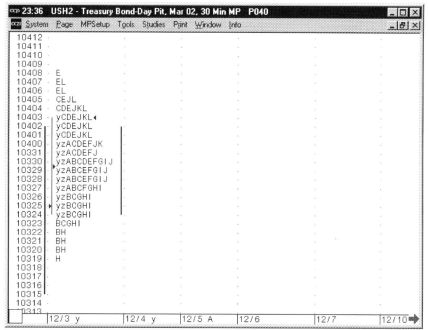

Figure 6–8   Market Profile display of the U.S. Treasury bond showing a neutral day.
Copyright © 1984 Chicago Board of Trade. All Rights Reserved. CBOT Market Profile, Market
Profile, Liquidity Data Bank, and LDB are registered trademarks of the Chicago Board of Trade.
All Rights Reserved. Provided by CQG.

ronment for continuation. In Figure 6–7, the profile for February
1 (2/1) illustrates a trend day. The market opened at the low of
its range for the day and closed near the high. Notice also that
the market held directional integrity to the upside (higher highs
and higher lows) and had single prints within the day.

The fifth basic classification of days is the neutral day. This
is a day in which the long-term traders exert opposite or con-
flicting influences. On the typical neutral day, both upside and
downside range extensions occur, netting out to little or no price
change for the day. The psychology behind the neutral day is
quite interesting. As we know, range extensions are a function of
the longer-term trader participation. On neutral days, both
longer-term buyer and seller involvement in the same range of
prices is an indication of their uncertainty. The profile displayed
in Figure 6–8 would be categorized as a neutral day.

A few observations made over time pertaining to the standard neutral day are symmetry in range extensions and propensity for a close near the middle of the day's range. In talking about symmetry in range extensions, I mean the range extension above the first hour's range is approximately the same number of ticks as the range extension below the first hour's range. The neutral day in Figure 6–8 displays this symmetrical characteristic. The first hour's range during y and z periods was expanded by 5 ticks to the upside and 5 ticks to the downside. Thus, the buyers' and sellers' commitment, or more specifically lack of commitment, is about equal. Buyers and sellers committing to an idea and not getting a payoff are the reasons for the phenomenon of closing near the middle of the day's range. This indecisiveness of the buyers and sellers also creates the self-fulfilling prophecy of neutral days begetting neutral days. There is no strong conviction by the longer-term participant, therefore they get involved, see no follow through, and get out. The opposite biased participant does the same thing, causing a preponderance of neutral days.

A derivative of the neutral day is the running profile neutral day. As in the standard neutral day, one sees longer-term participants expand price activity above and below the initial balance. The most significant difference between the running profile neutral day and the standard neutral day is the magnitude of the range extension and proximity of the close to the day's extreme. One will find that either the buyers or the sellers have more of an ax to grind, allowing for a settlement price near the day's high or low. Quite often, this day can signify change in trend. Essentially a running profile neutral day is 2 days rolled into 1. Figure 6–9, Cisco Systems, is an example of a running profile neutral day for January 9. The daily profile has been segmented accordingly. Note that during the first two-thirds of the day, the market expanded above the first hour's range by a few ticks and then started trading sideways. During the last three time periods of the day, the market sold off sharply. Thus the main difference between the two—the standard neutral day typically will have somewhat "balanced" range extensions whereas the running profile neutral day usually has a skew in one direction. The skew (or latest biggest move) typically is a precursor to continued price movement in that direction. The Cisco example held true to form: following the weak

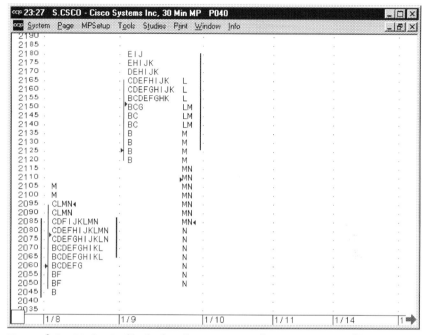

Figure 6–9 Market Profile display of Cisco Systems showing running profile neutral day segmented on January 9.

Copyright © 1984 Chicago Board of Trade. All Rights Reserved. CBOT Market Profile, Market Profile, Liquidity Data Bank, and LDB are registered trademarks of the Chicago Board of Trade. All Rights Reserved. Provided by CQG.

close of $20.85 on January 9, the market rallied 50 cents the next day and then broke $3.00 over the next 7 days.

Almost any trading day will fall into one of these classifications—nontrend day, normal day, normal variation day, trend day, or neutral day. Each involves a different set of likely range parameters, produced by a particular imbalance between short-term and long-term traders. If one can make the correct classification as the day develops, one can project how far the market is likely to move and create trading opportunities.

Table 6–1 contains what I call the matrix of day structure. Its purpose is to assist you in understanding the horizontal/vertical relationship between different day types. We often call this relationship between horizontal and vertical the degree of efficiency. A market with more horizontal or locked-in price control is called efficient. A market in more of a vertical phase—moving

Table 6–1   Matrix of Day Structure

| Day Type | Degree of Horizontal | | | |
	More Horizontal	→ → →		Less Horizontal
Nontrend	XX			
Normal		XX		
Normal variation			XX	
Trend				XX
Neutral		XX		
Running profile neutral			XX	

out of a price control area, more expansive—is called inefficient. The day types are listed in rows on the left side of the table. The columns to the right have double X's opposite the day type, reflective of the degree of horizontal in the daily profile. The further the X's are to the left the "fatter" (more horizontal) the profile. The further the X's are to the right, the "thinner" (less horizontal) the profile. Efficiency is signaled by X's on the left side of the table, and inefficiency is denoted by X's on the right side of the table.

From a daily Market Profile perspective, the beginning and end of the trading day create a market-imposed timeframe. There is a defined beginning and ending of the structure: a reference point from which to initiate positions and liquidate positions for those wishing to avoid overnight risk. When the psychology of the participants is incorporated with the time constant, one is able to utilize the measurement tools of the day structure. By using the initial balance as a gauge, one is able to measure stopping points for day structure. In stocks, for instance, this chronological profile would begin at 9:30 A.M. and finish at 4:00 P.M. EST. The initial balance would be from 9:30 to 10:30 A.M. EST. Following the first hour's trade (initial balance), the longer-term participants will expand the range higher or lower depending on their perspective of value relative to price. Based on the first hour's range and an understanding of day structure, one is able to project potential stopping points within the day.

One is able to apply this same concept and measurement tool as discussed earlier when looking at the market from a longer-term perspective. For instance, a logical starting point for the fixed income markets might be the day of the quarterly or monthly refunding. For the energy markets, one might want to look at the American Petroleum Institute (API) stats, American Gas Association (AGA) numbers for natural gas, or earnings reports for stocks. That point in time is used as a reference point pertaining to the initial balance for that contract. Price activity then expands that range and one is able to project future price objectives based on the assumptions presented earlier in describing day types.

For instance, consider 2 days as the initial balance for contracts having significant reports on a weekly basis. We will look at March West Texas Intermediary (WTI) traded on the New York Mercantile Exchange (NYMEX) as our example. The API report is released at 4:00 P.M. EST on Tuesday. The 2-day initial balance would be from 4:00 P.M. Tuesday to 4:00 P.M. Thursday. The expansion above/below this range would signify strong buying/selling measured against the range of the initial balance to project stopping points. For this example, let us look at Figure 6–10 with January 9th and 10th as the initial balance. For those 2 days, the range was $20.35 to $21.95 or $1.60 (owing to display limitations, we are unable to show prices in this example above $21.28). Calculating the initial balance range allows for projection of stopping levels based on the understanding of structure. However, in this case, weekly structure not day structure is discussed. Based on the 160-tick weekly initial balance and realizing that the market expanded lower, one is able to project stopping levels for a normal week or normal variation week. A normal week which is a 50 percent expansion of the 160-tick ($1.60) initial balance would be 80 ticks. A normal variation week would expand the 160-tick range by 100 percent (160 ticks). Thus knowing the low of the initial balance to be $20.35, it is possible to calculate a normal week to $19.55 ($20.35 − .80) or a normal variation week to $18.75 ($20.35 − 1.60). In this example, the low of the 5-day structure was $19.30, which slightly exceeded the objective of a normal week by some 25 ticks. Not bad, considering the range for those 5 days was 260 ticks.

Conceptually, what I am doing is moving farther and farther away from the trees to get a clear picture of the forest. Schultz's minimum trend concept creates a profile of the smallest working

```
23:44  CLH2 - Crude Light-Pit, Mar 02, 30 Min (Delayed by 30 mins) MP   P040
System  Page  MPSetup  Tools  Studies  Print  Window  Info
2128 | D
2121 | DE
2114 | CDEF
2107 | CDEFG
2100 | CDFGH
2093 | CFGHI      K
2086 | CGHIJ      K
2079 | HIJK       K            C
2072 | HJK        CDEK         CDEFG
2065 | JK         CDEGK        CDEFGHJ
2058 | K          CDEFGHK      CDEFGHIJK
2051 | K          CDEFGHIJK    DEIJK
2044 |            CDFGHIJK     DEIJK
2037 |            FHIJ         JK
2030 |            I            K
2023 |                         K
2016 |                         K
2009 |
2002 |                                 C
1995 |                                 C
1988 |                                 CDEF
1981 |                                 CDEF       J
1974 |                                 DEFK       DEFGIJK
1967 |                                 DEFGK      CDEFGHIJK
1960 |                                 FGHIK      CDEGHIK
1953 |                                 GHIK       CGHK
1946 |                                 GHIJK      CK
1939 |                                 HIJK       CK
1932 |                                 IJK
1925 |                                 J
1918 |
        1/9       1/10       1/11      1/14       1/15       1/16
```

Figure 6–10   Crude Light, March.

part of the market. From this, one is able to extrapolate larger and larger pieces of information until some macro profile is created.

For an example of a macro profile, look at the 30-year Treasury bond traded at the CBOT. Since its inception in 1977, the 30-year (adjusted for a 6% coupon) has traded between 58.00 and 112.00 (give or take a few points). If a graphic of this price activity were created, the profile would look much like a normalized bell curve: a preponderance of trade toward the middle of the price range and less toward the extremes (highs and lows). In these macro profiles, what typically puts these extremes in place is a news-driven event or fundamental change. Coincidentally, both affected the 30-year Treasury bond toward the end of 2001. The September 11 terrorist attack was the news-driven event and discontinuing issuance of 30-year debt was the change in fundamentals. This caused a spike to 113 on the nearby futures contract, creating an extreme.

From a statistical standpoint, one can calculate the third standard deviation of a contract by knowing the total range a market has traded since inception and that approximately 2.5 percent at either "tail" accounts for the third standard deviation. Subtracting the life-of-contract low of 58.00 from the high of 112.00 gives a total range of 54 points for the treasury bonds. The 2.5 percent tail would equal about 1.35 points on the Treasury bond. Thus, the spike of 1 + points over the life-of-contract high falls within the third standard deviation for the bond contract. Owing to limitations in software applications and publishing issues, it is not possible to create a huge composite profile of the bonds since they were launched in the early 1980s. Instead, a 2-month profile has been created to help illustrate the point (see Fig. 6–11). Hopefully the idea is conveyed in a manner that helps the reader conceptualize the thought.

This trade into and above the third standard deviation of the existing macro profile created a great selling opportunity for those looking at the market from a very long-term perspective. However, this push to new contract highs could have been a buy signal for people trading a short-term program. That is what makes markets and explains why there are buyers and sellers at every price. The shorter-term player sees a momentum play to the upside that he or she buys and the macro trader sees historically high prices that she or he sells because they should not be accepted over time.

This example is a great segue into coactive time frames. Coactive time frames are the push and pull that occur in all markets as people trade the market with different durations in mind. As long as historical data exist, traders are able to gauge current prices against historical prices and determine whether this current price is at, above, or below value relative to the time frame they wish to trade. Is there an opportunity?

Creating these longer-term chronological profiles requires nothing but a little creativity and observational skills. I call them chronological because some standardized point of reference is used for the beginning and end of a profile (i.e. weekly, between quarterly refundings, between earnings reports . . .). The

```
Capital Flow 3.76                                                    _ □ ×
Contract  Page  Display  Navigate  Study  Window  Utility  Feed  Scan  Help
Points  1: 12/13/2001 (y)                                           _ □ ×
10510    yzABE
10505    DJyBCEFJ
10500    yzABCDFGHJKLyCFGHIJKLyH
10427    JyzBEFHIJzAFHKLFGHyzACDFyFGHyIJLCDE
10422    JyJKLyzADFGGzDEFGJKLyzADEFGyzABFHIKLyzEFLGyzBCE
10417   *IJLJKLyABDEFGHIJABDABCDEFGHyzABCDELyzABCDEFGKLGHKyzAB
10412    IJKLGABCDyDEFGHKLyzBCDIJKLzDEFGHIJKFGHIJKL
10407    IyzEFGHIBHIJKyKyzABCDEFGIKyCDEHI
10402    GHIJyzABCDFIHIJKyBCKLyzABC
10329    GHJKLyACIIJBHJFFGHILyzB
10324    ABFGJKLyABCHIJKLyzEFGHFHyB
10319    ABCEKLyzABCDEHKLyzABCLDIKLyBCDEF
10314    AKyzABDyBDEFGzBCDEJKLyzCyzABCD
10309    AEJKKLyDEFIyzABCyzAB
10304    zABCEFGILCHIJKFHBA
10231    ABIJKLyzBCEGHILyBCDFGHIJGH
10226    DEAByyCDEFGIJyzyzAFG
10221    ADFGHyzABCyzyzBCDyy
10216    zACyzBCDLyzyA
10211    yzAByzAEFGICyDFABCDEFGHJKLyAGL
10206    yzBCDEGLyABCDEFHJKLyBCCFGHyABEFGAEGHIJKL
10201    yDEFFGHILBLyDEFyLyyzCGHyzBBCE
10128    EFGyzBACDEGILHyLyzKLyHLyBC
10123    FGKLyzBCEABKBCDJKLHAHCDEHJKzABEGJLIJKLB
10118    FGIJLyzACEFzABCDJKLBKACHILEFGHBCIB
10113    IJyFGHKyzBEHIKyzAABCBH
10108    IGLyzJLyzBFGyzAyzA
10103    LyzAIJKLy
10030    yyABCDEFHI
10025    yABFGH
10020    yzABCL
10015    ACDFKL
10010    GHIJK
10005    GHIJ
10000    ----
```

Figure 6–11   Two-month profile.

theory has evolved and moved away from chronological time to a market-generated time continuum that is called market time.

Four Steps of Market Activity

This market-generated continuum can be clearly explained using what is called the four Steps of Market Activity. It is the process markets go through to factor out inefficiencies. Inefficiencies are defined as the directional move, money flow, or distribution that propel prices sharply higher or lower within a defined amount of time. This viewpoint can be from a micro or a macro perspective. It is a visualization process that can be applied to any bar chart under any resolution. In other words, one

can monitor a 5-minute, 30-minute, daily, or any duration in between and visualize this phenomenon. It is one of the most important, if not the most important, skill a trader must learn and
apply to be successful. The four steps are:

Step 1 Series of prices in one direction
Step 2 Trade to a price to stop the market
Step 3 Develop around that stopping price
Step 4 Move to efficiency (retracement)

Step 1, which is a series of prices in one direction (often
called a distribution), could be the function of an economic number and therefore have a life of only a few minutes or it could be
a far more significant event that lasts a number of days or longer.
The second step in this cycle is the stopping phase. This does not
necessarily mean the market cannot trade higher or lower than
the stopping level, it means only the expansion phase has run its
course and momentum should be waning. The third step is the
development phase, which signals some degree of acceptance
around the stopping price. In some time frame, it would be defined as the first standard deviation. Finally, step 4 is an attempt
for the market to move to efficiency, in other words retrace some
of step 1 and move the first standard deviation back toward the
middle of the vertical range of the structure. A structure with a
completed step 4 would look like a normalized bell curve. However, the markets do not make things easy and at times the market can skip step 4 and continue in the same direction as step 1.
At other times, the steps are shortened or skipped all together.
Once again I want to emphasize how important it is conceptually to understand this four-step process and be able to visualize
the process in day-to-day trading. The reader who can accomplish this task will move far along the curve of becoming a successful trader, guaranteed!

In trading, major fundamental and/or economic events occur
with some degree of regularity and these events often signal
change. Some recent events include Russian grain embargo, de-
valuation of the Mexican peso, falling of the Berlin Wall, Desert
Storm, and the War on Terrorism. Some of these events were
commodity-specific; others affected the entire economic spec-

trum. This change in psychology is the natural beginning of a longer-term profile, one that is constructed via market time as opposed to chronological time. Market time means something that is free forming, it does not necessarily fall within the confines of the hour, day, or other time frame. It may begin with Alan Greenspan mumbling "irrational exuberance," a change in the weather forecast to include rain in the middle of a drought, or the International Monetary Fund (IMF) bailing out a Third World country down on their luck.

These events can occur at any time of the day or night; thus, the beginning of the structure does not have to coincide with the start of the day. Nor does the event need to be of such biblical proportions as those listed previously. They may be nothing more than a minor economic event or a larger player getting involved in a position. The life of the structure (profile) may be minutes, hours, days, or more.

As children growing up, all of us have memories of playing sandlot ball or learning how to ride a bike or swing a golf club. The teacher was probably one of our parents, an older sibling, or the kid in the neighborhood who seemed to be good at everything. Over time, we became more and more proficient at our chosen activities through day-to-day involvement or practice. This process of self-discovery is ultimately responsible for all of our achievements, no matter how large or small.

In learning, the cursory overview is followed by clumsy attempts that evolve into more fluidity and ultimately accomplishment. The light goes on; "I got it" is exclaimed. I can hit that baseball, ride that bike, and do that long division. The amount of time needed to reach this stage varies based on the task involved and the ability of the individual. Some people are naturals; others are relentless in their efforts, yet things come to them more slowly.

Once a person becomes accomplished at something, it becomes second nature and she or he needs to look internally to understand all the mechanics of what goes into the task. Through great amounts of inner and external observation, this accomplished person may be able to take a leap forward and become a teacher, verbalize the process.

Market Profile and we as teachers of the methodology have gone through a similar "evolution." In the early stages of our trading careers, we had some ideas that we felt had a sound foundation (bell curve). We pumped exchange data into this graphic display to create the Market Profile. The problem was there was no one out there with the ability to show us how to use the tool. Self-discovery in its most basic form was necessary to expand our knowledge base and grow. We pursued the task with enthusiasm and vigor. There was no blueprint in place. At times, we reached a fork in the road and went down the wrong path, needing to backtrack and find our way again. Now some 20 years after its introduction to the trading community, we are finally in a position to verbalize the concepts.

Internal Time Clock of the Market

A logical progression or evolution of the four steps of market activity is the internal time clock of the market. Understanding and applying this concept will improve one's trading from a timing standpoint. Knowing the different thresholds or breakpoints of the internal time clock of the market will allow the reader to more objectively measure the four steps of market activity.

What is the internal time clock of the market? It is a tool developed to measure the recurrence of prices traded over time. How does it work? It looks at the timeslots used or total number of letters accumulated across the wide TPO point of the data mass being measured and assigns that number to the structure. Figure 6–12 is a display of the July soybeans. Laser lines (proprietary study generated off Capital Flow 3.76) have been generated for two individual composite profiles for the purpose of displaying the wide TPO point of the structure. The wide TPO point for each structure is referenced with the solid horizontal line across the profile. The number of letters within the shaded horizontal line is the TPO count for the structure. Counting the number of TPOs across the first structure, one finds there are 24 TPOs; across the second profile, there are 14 TPOs. Through observation over time, this information has been quantified to help de-

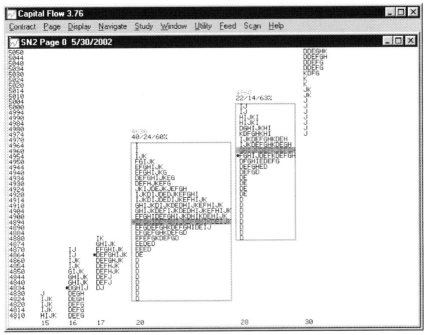

Figure 6–12   Display of July soybeans with the laser lines.

termine whether the market is in a condition for continuation or change (nonrandom or random).

Recall that the four steps of market activity:

Step 1 Series of prices in one direction
Step 2 Trade to a price to stop the market
Step 3 Develop around that stopping price
Step 4 Attempt to move the first standard deviation (stopping and developing prices) back toward the middle of the vertical range of the structure

The internal time clock of the market can be used to objectively tell where one is within this process. We categorized the time-slots used (wide TPO point of structure) to assist us in determining the four steps.

Timeslots-Used Matrix

0–18 timeslots used	Trend continuation
19–29 timeslots used	Market has reached level of containment, therefore in step 3
30–42 timeslots used	Normal development time for step 3 and change to step 1, which could be in same direction as original step 1 or could be counter to original step 1, which by default is step 4
43–75 timeslots used	Market has reached a state of overdevelopment and prices should move opposite the direction it took to get there

Note that these numbers should not be seen as absolutes. For instance, markets that are more volatile may see development times shortened by as much as 20 percent across the board; similarly, markets that are relatively static and have less trading interest may have development times increased by as much as 20 percent.

Now that the reader has a general understanding of what to look for when measuring the internal time clock of the market, let us work through an example to reinforce the concept. Within the Capital Flow 3.76 universe, we suggest leaving a laser line study open-ended to be cognizant of where the current development is within the internal time clock of the market. Figure 6–13 is a daily profile display of the September Municipal Bond Index traded on the CBOT. The data will be manipulated to help the reader understand how to work with the internal time clock of the market. In Figure 6–14, a few days of profiles have been combined to create a composite profile with a laser line study overlaying the composite unit. The wide TPO point of the profile is 11 at the price is 101.04. In the upper left-hand corner of the laser line overlay is the pertinent information to the internal time clock of the market: the actual price at the wide TPO point of the structure and the timeslots used for the internal time clock of the market. The top number indicates the price of the wide TPO, where the laser line is af-

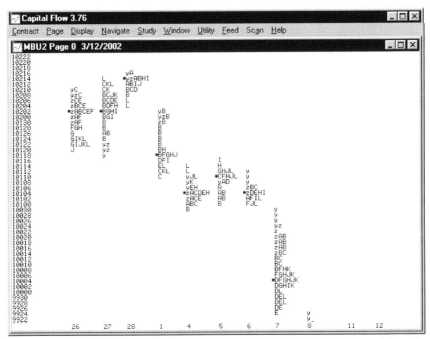

Figure 6–13 Daily profile display of the September Municipal Bond Index traded on the Chicago Board of Trade.

Copyright © 1984 Chicago Board of Trade. All Rights Reserved. CBOT Market Profile, Market Profile, Liquidity Data Bank, and LDB are registered trademarks of the Chicago Board of Trade. All Rights Reserved. Provided by Steidlmayer Software Inc.

fixed to the structure. Below this number is a series of three numbers, the first of which is the total number of half-hours in the structure, the second number indicates the number of half-hour bars along the laser line or wide TPO point of the structure (the number used within the internal time clock of the market). Looking at our timeslots-used matrix, the current reading of 11 timeslots used falls within the trend continuation mode for the measured structure.

Figure 6–15 shows how the market continues to expand vertically to the downside with no additional horizontal development. With the market trading near 99 even, our wide TPO count still sits at 101.04. As more data are brought into the analysis, Figure 6–16 illustrates continued price erosion to the down-side and that the laser line has shifted to a lower price of 99.15. The internal time clock of the market measurement stands at 14, indicating trend continuation. Adding a few more days into the analysis, in Figure 6–17 the laser line or wide TPO point has moved a few ticks lower to 99.12. The total number of half-hours or the internal time clock of the market has reached 22, moving out of trend continuation and into containment based on our timeslots-used matrix.

As more data are brought into the structure, Figure 6–18 shows a clearly defined 3:2:1 to the downside. Based on the four steps of market activity, there is a series of prices in one direc-tion, trading to a price to stop the market (99.12), and we have

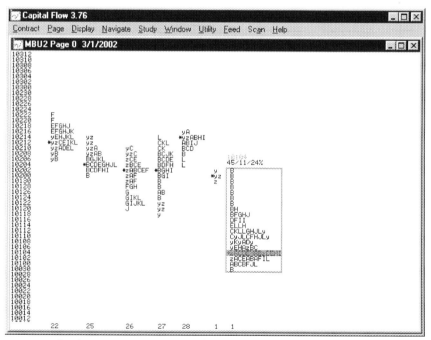

Figure 6–14   Time/price opportunity (TPO) Composite Profile highlighted with box.

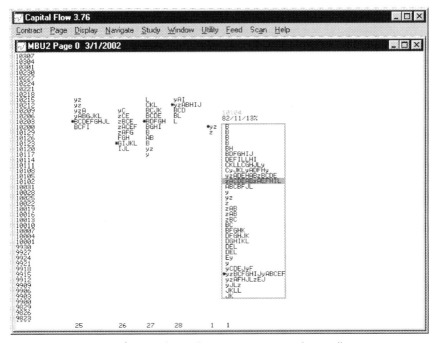

Figure 6–15   The market continues to expand vertically.

developed around the stopping price. Looking at the four steps, one would now expect the market to try to move this stopping price back toward the middle of the vertical price range of this structure. Seeing the stopping and development occurring, the logical question would be, when can one look for this backing and filling to occur? Based on the internal time clock of the market 30 to 42 time slots used is the normal development time for step 3 and a move to step 4. With the internal time clock of the market reading 40, this market is ripe for some type of reversal from a timing standpoint. A strategy might be to initiate a long position once the market starts to rally above the laser line (wide TPO point) or possibly sell puts on the breaks, knowing the market is due to trade sideways at worst.

Owing to space limitations, I have moved from a profile display to bar chart display and left the laser line study on the chart for reference purposes (Fig. 6–19). Moving to a bar chart display, the horizontal depth a profile affords the user is lost; however, I think a simple visualization exercise will convey the rest of the story. The vertical bar with the box around it represents the big composite profile that has been used to monitor the internal time clock of the market. Reaching a maturity level of 40 has one looking for backing and filling to occur. Looking at the bar chart, one can see that is exactly what happened from the time the laser line study was closed off. For the following 3 weeks, prices pushed away from the wide TPO point of 99.12 and never retested that price.

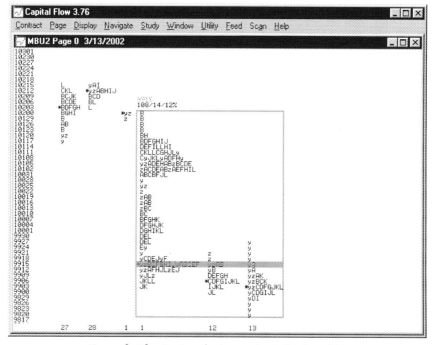

Figure 6–16   Continued price erosion to the downside.

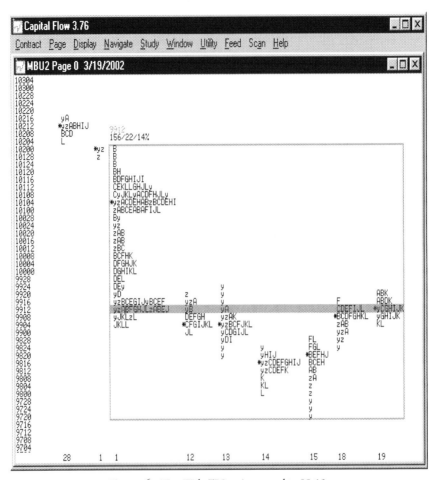

Figure 6–17   Wide TPO point moved to 99.12.

Understanding that out of price control comes non–price control, one should be able to become proficient at recognizing when a market has entered the distribution process and thus "turn on the clock" to assist in determining where one is within the development matrix. A thought process I encourage traders to develop is looking for endings as opposed to beginnings. By default, is not an ending also some sort of beginning? If one has a tool to assist in determining when the structure is complete, isn't one a step ahead of the game, sitting in a position knowing that volatility should come back into the market? Taking this one step further based on the four steps of market activity, one should be able to make an educated guess on direction. At that point, one can trade the underlying or use options to implement a strategy.

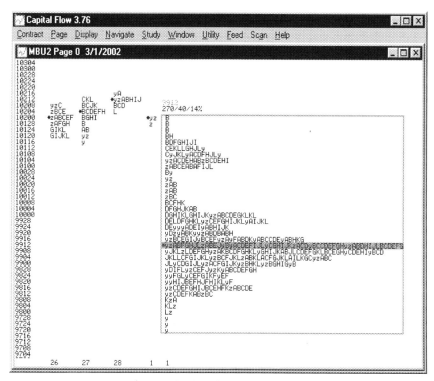

Figure 6–18   Clearly defined 3:2:1 to the downside.

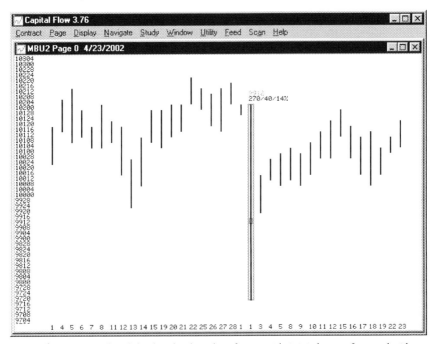

Figure 6–19   Muni bond displayed in bar chart format with 3:2:1 down referenced with large box around price activity.

Provided by Steidlmayer Software Inc.

Beyond-The-Day Activity

The beyond-the-day trader will be buying or selling at different price areas in the market; and we know, from experience, that long-term traders do not make a habit of trading with one another but almost always with the day traders, locals or specialists. Some of the participants in the commodity world who would be categorized as longer-term or commercial traders who seldom trade with one another would be the end-user and the producer. Look to the grain markets for an example and focus on corn specifically and use the Midwestern farmer as the producer and General Mills as the end-user. The criterion for when to get involved is different for both parties. The producer (farmer) wants to sell at the highest price possible to realize the most profits from the crop, and the end-user (General Mills) wants to buy as cheaply as possible to produce the finished good at a competitive price. The dynamics of each of their operations is different. Yet the goal is the same—turn a profit. The variables affecting the profitability of the farmer can range from costs of fertilizer, petroleum, and labor; the unknowns of weather; yield; and demand. The variables affecting the end-user can range from availability and cost of substitutes, cost of labor, and selling price of finished good. The polarity at which these two parties approach the market does not encourage the direct trade of commercial to commercial. On average, it is not a win/win situation. When the grain prices are low, the end-user gains and the producer loses; when the grains are highly priced, the producer benefits and the end-user loses. This is not a business model that allows for much staying power by either participant. That is where the intermediaries come into play. The local, day trader, and position trader create liquidity and direction, which create the volatility that allows producers and end-users to participate at prices that are more palatable.

So one needs to be able to look at the range and development of the Market Profile and extract from it the long-term trader's activity. The long-term trader will be active throughout the profile, so one needs to examine the profile in its entirety not to miss any information.

Let us start by defining some important terms that will help us understand the long-term activity. The first term is an extreme. An extreme is activity at the top or bottom of the price range represented by two or more TPOs (single prints on the profile) by themselves. An extreme results when there is a directional bias in the market and the opposite participant comes into the market and overwhelms the existing direction. In this scenario, an extreme is left in the market. An extreme cannot occur in the last period of the day because there is no successive trade against which to test. By definition, an extreme is a price that the market has tested, then moved away from quickly or rejected. A term synonymous with extreme is buying tail and selling tail. The buying tail would be the single prints below the first standard deviation; the selling tail the single prints above the first standard deviation. The word tail came into being because visually the first standard deviation of a profile looks like the "body" and single prints the "tail."

Figure 6–20, Tribune Company, contains some examples of extremes, together with some patterns that might resemble extremes but that do not really fit our definition. The elements labeled 1, 2, 3, and 4 in the figure are extremes. Each is a series of two or more TPOs that the market moved away from as an unfair price. Conversely, the element labeled 5 is not an extreme because it occurred during the last time period for trading—these prices could not be tested by any successive trade so it is not categorized as an extreme. Finally, the print labeled 6 is not an extreme because it is a single tick at the low of the profile. An extreme, by definition, must be two or more ticks and cannot occur during the last session of the day.

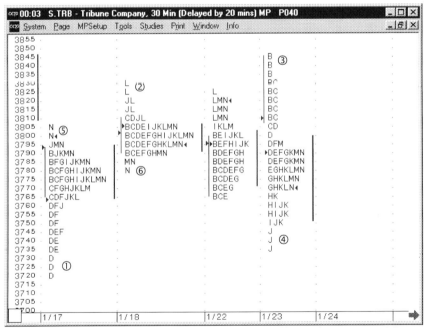

Figure 6–20   Tribune Company with extremes denoted by numbers 1, 2, 3 and 4.

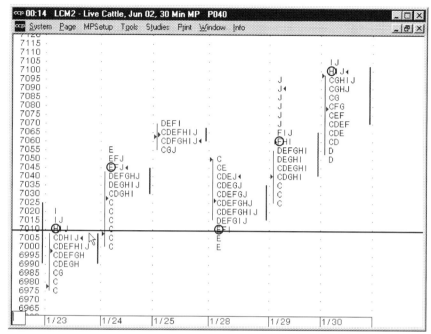

Figure 6–21   Live cattle with daily auction points circled.

Another important term is range extension. A range extension is any extension in the day's price range that occurs beyond the first hour of trading. What causes the range extension above/below the initial balance is longer-term buyers/sellers getting involved in the market because they believe prices to be too cheap/expensive, respectively. In Figure 6–21, the first hour's trading for each day is represented by the C and D prints. The point at which the range extension occurred each day is indicated by the circled print and is called the auction point. In each case, this was the first TPO for the day located beyond the first hour's range. The auction point, or the specific point in time and price at which longer-term buyers or sellers step into the market, is an important piece of information. It is the starting point for measuring the supplemental range parameters that allows one to project objectives for day structure. Additionally, this auction point up or auction point down should serve as support or resistance, respectively, until it is tested at some later time. The live cattle display in Figure 6–21 supplies a better understanding of how the auction point works. The first profile displayed has a range extension above the first hour's range at 7010. This is called our auction point to the upside and a horizontal line has been drawn across the screen at this price to give a reference point of support for later trade. The next day, the market opens up unchanged and trades down through the auction point by a tick or two and then reverses and closes higher. A few days later, the market again comes down and tests the auction point to the upside and the market holds once again. Generally, one wants to be loose in interpretations of price activity because trading is not an exact science. As long as the market does not violate an auction point by a significant amount and as long as it continues to close in the auction direction, the level is good.

The last term covered in this section is TPO count. A TPO is created each time a new price occurs during one of the trading day's half-hour time periods. Collectively, these TPOs make the daily profile. To find the TPO count for any given day, first locate the price with the greatest number of TPOs nearest the middle of the range (fattest part of profile). Then count the number of TPOs (total letters) above and below this line. The result is the TPO count. The premise is that profiles eventually build into some type of a normalized bell curve. Thus, if there are more letters below the wide point of the profile, TPO buying occurs and the price activity should "roll" higher and spend time building TPOs above the wide TPO line to create a normalized bell curve. Conversely, if there are more letters above the wide TPO line, TPO selling exists and subsequent price activity should roll down and develop below the wide TPO point to create some type of a normalized bell curve.

The March 2-year note will provide some insight on how to interpret the TPO count. In Figure 6–22, I have drawn a horizontal line across the wide TPO point for the profile on January 25. In a box at the bottom of the page is the corresponding TPO count for that day's activity. If the price scale were changed to one tick for the contract and the total number of TPOs above and below the wide TPO point counted, there would be 57 buying

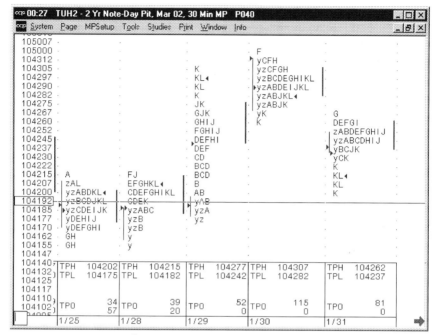

Figure 6–22   Two-year note with TPO counts shown.

Copyright © 1984 Chicago Board of Trade. All Rights Reserved. CBOT Market Profile, Market Profile, Liquidity Data Bank, and LDB are registered trademarks of the Chicago Board of Trade. All Rights Reserved. Provided by CQG.

TPOs and 34 selling TPOs (the TPO count is shown in the box below the profile opposite the word TPO; the bottom number signifies buying TPOs and the top number selling TPOs). If the cursor continues to move over the wide TPO point for each profile, the next two profiles would also have buying TPO counts of 38/14 and 72/32 for January 28 and 29, respectively. These numbers are not displayed in the TPO count because the cursor is not over the wide TPO point for the given profiles. In other words, for 3 consecutive days the buyer dominated and the prices worked higher. On the fourth profile of Figure 6–22, which also happens to be the first profile on Figure 6–23, notice the TPO count has moved from buying to selling. In Figure 6–23, this is determined by drawing a horizontal line across the widest TPO point nearest the middle of the day's range for the profile dated January 30. By looking at the box below the daily profile, one can

```
co 00:42   TUH2 - 2 Yr Note-Day Pit, Mar 02, 30 Min MP   P040         _ □ ×
 co  System  Page  MPSetup  Tools  Studies  Print  Window  Info        _ 8 ×
 105005
 105000 ·  F                       ·
 104315 ►  yCF                     ·
 104310 ·  yzCFGH                  ·
 104305 ·  yzCFGH                  ·
 104300 ·  yzBCDEGHIKL             |
 104295 ·  yzABDEIKL               |
 104290 ◄►yzABDEIJKL────────────────────────────
 104285 ·  yzABJKL◄               |
 104280 ·  yzABJK                 |
 104275 |  yzBK
 104270 |· yK               ·  G
 104265 |· K                ·  G
 104260 |· K                   DEFGI
 104255 |·                     ADEFGHIJ     |
 104250 |·                  ·| zABDFHIJ      ·
 104245 |·                     yzABCHIJ     ·
 104240 ·                    ►| yBCJK        |
 104235 ·                    ·►yBCJK
 104230 ·                  ·  K
 104225 ·                  ·  K
 104220 ·                  ·  KL◄
 104215 ·                  ·  KL
 104210 ·                  ·  KL
 104205 ·                  ·  K
 104200 ·                  ·  K             ·
 104195 | TPH   104307     | TPH   104262
 104190 | TPL   104282     | TPL   104237
 104185 |
 104180 |
 104175 | TPO       59     | TPO        0
 104170 |           46     |           81
        |  1/30            |  1/31
```

Figure 6–23   Two-year note showing TPO selling on January 30.

see that the TPO count is 59 selling TPOs and 46 buying TPOs. On balance, the day was a selling day and one can expect prices to try to trade lower. On the next day, expectations are met as the market has a decent selloff.

By monitoring extremes, range extension, and the TPO count for any developing market, one can gain a sense of what long-term traders are doing. As long as the activity of the beyond-the-day traders is unbalanced, the price level will tend to maintain itself or move directionally. For instance, 5 consecutive days of activity with 10 buys and 3 sells (activities we are measuring are extremes, range extensions and TPO's for each of the 5 days) will mean that the market should hold its price, if not move higher. Conversely, if there were 3 buys and 10 sells, one would expect to see prices either remain the same or fall.

As the reader can see by combining an understanding of the day time frame and beyond-the-day disciplines, the lever that causes market activity to increase or decrease is the raising or lowering of prices. A large day time frame influence pushing prices down creates a good opportunity for the long-term trader to enter the market from the long side, assuming the trend has been up. By the same token, too large an imbalance of buying that ends a long-term market trend usually creates a good opportunity for the day trader because it will probably cause an excess in the market place once it moves away from those prices. This is called trapped money. The rally in the 30-year Treasury bonds following the terrorist attack and government discontinuing issuance of 30-year debt is a great example of a long-term excess. The market rallied from 102 to 112 over 2 months and broke back down to 104 in 2 weeks. The high established in this time frame could serve as an excess for many years to come.

Price cannot simultaneously serve two masters. This is the basic principle that creates opportunity for a trader.

Initiating Versus Responsive Activity

Understanding and distinguishing between these two types of activity are difficult for many traders. In this section, I give some tips that should help the reader deal with them conceptually and practically.

First, consider initiating and responsive activity as they relate to the previous day. Use the previous day's value area as a reference point. The value area is defined as the first standard deviation of that day's range. In other words, the value area should encompass approximately 68 percent of the day's volume or TPOs. It would necessarily include the widest part of the profile. For those not having access to a vendor-calculated value area or for those keeping profiles by hand, the calculation is quite simple. First count the total number of TPOs in the given profile and determine what 68 percent of that total would be. Next go to the profile graphic and locate the two consecutive prices that encompass the greatest number of TPOs nearest the middle of the days range. Finally, take the two consecutive prices above the wide TPO line and add the number of TPOs in that group. Do the same for the two consecutive prices below the wide TPO line. Compare the two group's totals and add the greater of the two to the existing TPO count. Continue this process until 68 percent of the total TPOs are accumulated—this is the TPO value area.

Next, reference the market activity of extremes, range extensions, and TPOs as they evolve in the newly developing day. The key is to track market activity above or below the previous day's value area. When today's activity is buying below the previous day's value area, this is responsive activity. So is selling above the previous day's value area. Participants are responding to "cheap" or "expensive" prices relative to previous day's activity. They are buying below value and selling above value. An example of buying below value would be walking into a favorite men's store and seeing Armani suits marked down 40 percent. Seeing this you would not tear off your own suit and chase down the sales assistant suggesting she or he purchase the suit from you at a 40 percent discount. No, that would not be a normal response; knowing your affinity for Armani, you would probably make a purchase realizing the suits were priced below value. Similarly, if someone knocked on your door and offered you twice your perceived value of your home, you would almost certainly sell to the prospective buyer. You are selling above value and you will handle the family's objections later.

By contrast, buying above the previous day's value area or selling below the previous day's value area is initiating activity. The reason for generating initiating trades is because participants perceive a shift in value. They are going with the flow. They believe the value of something has appreciated versus yesterday's activity; thus, they are willing to pay up to be long or they believe their trading vehicle has depreciated and they are willing to sell cheap versus yesterday's value area. Look in Figure 6–24 at the activity in Sony Corporation from January 18 through 24. The stock gapped lower on January 22 (1/22) and closed on the low. Not only did it open above the value area of January 22 on January 23, but it also gapped open and rallied for the next 2 days. This is the clear result of initiative buying on both the twenty-third and the twenty-fourth—buying above the

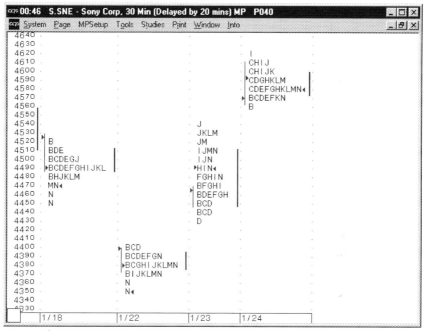

Figure 6–24 Daily Market Profile display of Sony Corporation showing initiating activity. Copyright © 1984 Chicago Board of Trade. All Rights Reserved. CBOT Market Profile, Market Profile, Liquidity Data Bank, and LDB are registered trademarks of the Chicago Board of Trade. All Rights Reserved. Provided by CQG.

previous day's value area; just as the January 22 activity was initiative selling—selling below the previous day's value area.

From a macro perspective, changes in technology are often great incentives for initiating activity. Can you imagine the impact computers with word processing capabilities had on the typewriter industry? I am sure the decreased demand forced distributors to sell their inventory below what had been a fair price. They were forced to become initiating sellers. Let us look at the impact hybrid seeds had on farming. The development of seeds that increased yields or were adaptable to harsher conditions caused farmland to appreciate. What was once "marginal land" now became revenue-producing and thus sold for a premium over what had been previously considered fair value.

The concepts of initiating and responsive activity can also be related to developments within the day. Simply refer to the first, second, and third standard deviations for the developing day. The market is described as initiating when it is in the second or third standard deviation; it is responsive in the first. This is illustrated in Chapter 9.

Excesses

An extreme is to an excess as a pond is to a lake. They both have the same makeup. One is just of a far grander scale than the other. Excesses can occur in many fashions. They are a useful tool in reading the market from both the short-term and the long-term viewpoint. Good floor traders learn to recognize excesses instinctively. They are usually characterized by fast, unanswered price movements in the market. Excesses become areas that constitute barriers to further price movement, and therefore make excellent reference points for the trader.

Figure 6–25 is a daily bar chart of Royal Dutch Petroleum that covers almost 6 months of price activity. In the chart, two excesses are referenced with the numbers 1 and 2. The impetus for the big selloff in September was the terrorist attack on New York City and the Pentagon, which culminated with a huge excess on September 24 (the number 1). It was clear that this represented an excess that would be a barrier to further trade on the low end for some time. In our second excess (the number 2), which occurred in mid-November, the magnitude of the break was not as great; however, the fact that the market opened lower, broke sharply, then rallied, and closed on the high for the day signaled another bottom, not of the same magnitude as the first, but a barrier to be traded against for the immediate future.

Market Profile and Spreads

Market Profile and its reference points are applicable for trading relationships between different commodities or stocks. A spread is a combined long and short position of two contracts. A trader can profit from a spread based on a change in the relationship be-

Figure 6–25   Royal Dutch Petroleum with excesses denoted.

Provided by CQG.

tween the underlying prices. If one is an experienced trader who likes to use spreads in the trading strategy, Market Profile can be used to find profit opportunities in "plain vanilla" spreads as well as any on or off the floor–traded instruments.

Figures 6–26 and 6–27 are Market Profiles of two different spread relationships. Figure 6–26 is a spread between the bund and the bobl (10-year and 5-year fixed-income instruments traded on Eurex). Notice the similarities between the spread profiles and the day structure discussed earlier in this chapter. Lowercase "k" and "l" represent the initial balance for these spreads. January 7 could be catagorized as a trend day followed by 2 parallel neutral days on January 8 and 9, followed by another trend day. This spread appears to be more directional and warrants a go-with approach. The next example (Fig. 6–27) is a spread between the Nasdaq 100 and the Standard and Poors 500—more of a mean reverting market. Knowing the characteristics of the

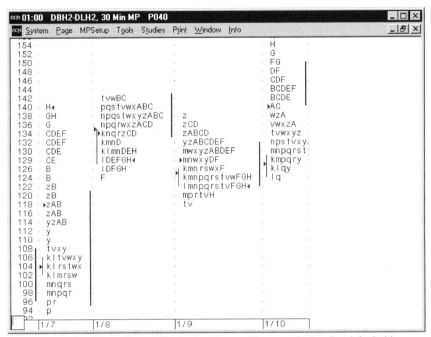

Figure 6–26   Market Profile display of spread between the bund and the bobl.

market one is trading (whether it be outright or spread trading) allows an approach with more of an initiating or a responsive strategy.

Market Profiles can be used for trading anything on an organized exchange or over the counter. Because the profile reflects the underlying nature of markets, which does not differ fundamentally from one market to another, the same basic methods can be applied no matter what contract, commodity, or product is being bought or sold.

As a trader, along with my knowledge and experience, I always had an intuitive "feel" for the market—an understanding that I could never quite quantify or express, yet could use in any developing market place. This intuitive insight involves sensing opportunities and catching their development as it happens. In the trading classes I teach, which are always conducted live as the day's markets are developing, I have often been able to make adjustments or see exceptions to the parameters and disciplines I set out for the students.

I reflected on this for quite some time and began to explore this intuitive aspect of trading. This ability is something that has developed over time, a function of one's involvement in the market. Never discount this intuitive feeling; always try to incorporate it into the trading platform.

The reader should try to utilize the objective information communicated by the Market Profile and incorporate or blend into that your own observations and experiences gained by sitting behind the screen, trading on the floor, or personal life experiences. We all have a wealth of information stored in our subconscious that can and should be tapped to make us more

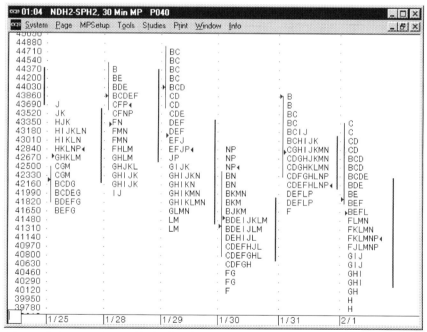

Figure 6–27 Market Profile display of spread between the Nasdaq 100 and the S&P 500. Copyright © 1984 Chicago Board of Trade. All Rights Reserved. CBOT Market Profile, Market Profile, Liquidity Data Bank, and LDB are registered trademarks of the Chicago Board of Trade. All Rights Reserved. Provided by CQG.

successful traders. One should move away from seeing everything as either black or white but instead open our eyes to all the
colors of the rainbow. To some degree, move trading from science to an art. We call this the natural way of trading.

Market Profile is simple in concept, but very complex in
detail. By contrast, the natural way of trading is very simple in detail, yet complex in theory. I believe the reader's time will be better spent focusing on the complexities of the theory than on any
mass of details. In the chapters that follow, I make a deliberate effort not to overload you with details. I do not want to overwhelm
with despair at the size of the hill you are about to climb. In this
section of the book, I have explained what Market Profile is and
the concepts behind it. I have presented a few of the basic definitions and parameters based on it. Later, in the portion of this book
dealing with trade preparation, I use these concepts to guide you
through techniques you can use in preparing for the day's trading.
The focus is on the natural way of trading and on how you can
gradually incorporate the additional information that comes from
Market Profile and volume analysis into your trading practices.

Chapter 7

LIQUIDITY DATA BANK, ON FLOOR INFORMATION, AND VOLUME @ TIME

Over the past 10 to 15 years, our industry has seen changes in technology, changes in market dynamics, and changes in our approach to reading volume. Initially, our focus was looking at Liquidity Data Bank (LDB) and trying to understand the nuances of the different categories of participants getting involved at certain prices. Next, we try to weigh their involvement and come to a decision on how it would affect the probability of continuation or change. At times, these numbers really stood out and this usually meant a clear-cut opportunity was at hand. However, most of the time the process was quite subjective owing to the similarity of numbers being compared and difficulty in weighing the different commodity trader identification (CTI) codes.

Thus, over time, we had to update our volume analysis. The three types of volume analysis available to Market Profile users today are LDB, on floor information (OFI), and volume @ time.

LDB is a volume report put out by the Chicago Board of Trade (CBOT) after the market closes. Its value lies in helping determine whether continuation or change in market activity is likely. The underlying assumption is that market behavior—mass human behavior—within the structure of the auction market is less likely to change on high volume than on low volume.

OFI is a statistic generated by the CBOT. OFI assists in understanding whether large orders generated off the exchange floor are more skewed toward the buy side or the sell side. The assumption being "the big barn boss" will attempt to defend his position (at least in the short term). This information is available after the market closes.

The last type of volume information available to Market Profile users is volume @ time. This information is readily available on all electronic futures exchanges and stock exchanges and is becoming more accessible on open outcry exchanges. What this volume sampling shows is the amount of volume occurring over a defined segment of time. If one is using the industry standard Market Profile, one would be looking at volume occurring in half-hour segments. One advantage this platform has over the other two is the timeliness of the information release. When available, LDB and OFI are released after the market closes; volume @ time is real time as the transaction occurs.

Owing to the fact LDB is available only on CBOT contracts, I offer only a cursory overview of the topic. A great deal of information is generated from the LDB report; however, I cannot justify dedicating a great amount of time and space to something that has such a limited scope. For those interested in getting an in-depth review of this topic please refer back to the original Steidlmayer on Markets or contact Don Jones@Cisco-futures.com.

Understanding the Liquidity Data Bank Report

To help the reader understand the LDB report, a sample printout is presented with all the salient points highlighted. Most of the information is self-explanatory (commodity name, expiration month and year, price, volume, % volume at a price, and time bracket). Now let's work on developing an understanding of CTI codes 1 to 4. The codes represent categories the exchange has created that allow participants to be given a specific designation. They are:

CTI-1 Local/specialist
CTI-2 Commercial trading for own account
CTI-3 Member trading off floor or having other member fill order
CTI-4 General public/funds

Essentially CTI-1 and CTI-3 equate to the local or specialist activity of creating liquidity or market making. On average, they account for 50 percent of the day's volume. This percentage will probably increase as side-by-side trading (floor and electronic trading simultaneously) becomes more prevalent. Local participation is a phenomenon that always needs to be present to make a contract vibrant and alive.

To simplify the process, one should focus on CTI-2 and CTI-4 when looking at LDB reports. CTI-2 represents the commercials trading for their own account and CTI-4 includes the general public and funds—the latter is our focus. Looking at these two categories will give the most reliable indicator when looking at LDB information. Focus on commercial and fund activity because they are opportunistic in their approach to trading. If they perceive price away from value, they will get involved, whereas the local or specialist attempts to be involved at every price. Thus, when CTI-2 participation is significantly higher than the norm, this involvement should be flagged and incorporated into one's thought process. They are trading more than normal because it is their belief that they are taking advantage of price away from value. They are selling at the high of the bell curve when the market is stretched to the upside; and conversely, they are buying at the low of the bell curve when the market is stretched to the downside.

Funds (CTI-4) participate at the extremes in just the opposite fashion. Funds play "go with"—in other words, when prices are high and they think they are going higher, funds will buy; if prices are low and they think they are going lower, funds will sell. This approach seems contrary to what logic would say but not really. They are buying high or selling low because they believe the market is undervalued or overvalued from more of a macro perspective; they believe a "shift in value" is on the horizon. Now look at an LDB report to get an understanding of what this is all about.

Figure 7–1 is an LDB report. The heading at the top indicates the report was generated for price activity on January 14, 2002. The next line shows that the commodity name is the T-bond and the expiration month is March 2002. Below these headings is all the volume summary information with CTI breakdowns. In the

```
CHICAGO BOARD OF TRADE                          LIQUIDITY DATA BANK* REPORT

                    VOLUME/FUTURES SUMMARY REPORT FOR 01 14 02

COMMODITY  --  T-BOND (CBOT) DAY        MAR 02


Volume Summary

        Price   Volume   %Vol %Cti1 %Cti2 %Cti3 %Cti4 Brackets
        10400       12    0.0  50.0   0.0   0.0  25.0 A
        10331     3554    2.5  60.6   3.0   2.3  34.2 ABEG
        10330     7042    5.0  55.4   4.7   6.0  33.9 ABDEG
        10329     8538    6.0  56.9   9.9   7.3  26.0 ABCDEFGH
        10328    12398    8.8  55.8   5.0   4.1  35.0 ABCDEFGH
        10327    11740    8.3  57.1   9.5   6.3  27.1 $ABCDEFGHI
        10326    17784   12.6  50.7   3.7   4.5  41.2 $ABCDEFGHI
        10325     8328    5.9  58.7   5.7   7.5  28.0 $ABCDEFHI
        10324    10032    7.1  59.1   5.2   6.8  28.9 $ABCDEFI
        10323     6638    4.7  64.4   6.5   8.1  21.0 $ABCEFI
        10322    11072    7.8  56.2   3.7   6.5  33.6 $ABCEFIJ
        10321     4904    3.5  66.9   5.3   5.5  22.3 $ABCEFIJ
        10320     2616    1.9  62.0   1.6   8.9  27.5 Z$CIJ
        10319     4254    3.0  61.1   2.9   9.1  26.8 Z$CIJ
        10318     2706    1.9  65.8   4.2   9.3  20.6 ZCIJ
        10317     3834    2.7  59.8   3.6   7.7  28.8 ZIJ
        10316     3210    2.3  57.9   3.5   8.0  30.6 ZJK
        10315     2322    1.6  58.2   0.1   5.0  36.6 ZJK
        10314     2868    2.0  64.8   0.0   6.5  28.7 JKL
        10313     3262    2.3  65.4   0.4   4.3  30.0 JKL
        10312     6396    4.5  52.2  11.0   6.1  30.6 KL
        10311     2712    1.9  61.5   2.8   7.1  28.6 KLM
        10310     1566    1.1  55.0   1.1   3.3  40.5 KLM
        10309     3090    2.2  58.3  15.8   8.1  17.9 LM
        10308      510    0.4  50.6   0.0   0.6  48.6 LM

70%     10330   101092   71.5  57.0   5.6   6.1  31.3 Z$ABCDEFGHIJ
V-A     10320
```

Figure 7–1   LDB report for 01 14 02 of the T-Bond.

left-most column are the prices traded for that day listed in descending order (104.00 to 103.08). The next column to the right displays the total number of contracts traded at each individual price. The next column to the right gives this same volume information as a percentage of the total volume for the day. The next four columns to the right of the %volume column list CTI codes 1 to 4, respectively, with the corresponding volume percentages for each price. The last column displays the brackets (as listed on the floor of the exchange) during the day the designated price traded—a Market Profile graphic. Below the array of prices with their corresponding information is found a row that lists the 70 percent volume value area (first standard deviation) and the aforementioned information that entails the 70 percent volume value area. In our example, the 70 percent volume value area range was from 103.20 to 103.30 and the total number of contracts traded in that range was 101,092. The volume%, CTI breakdown%, and time bracket breakdown are also given for this 70 percent volume value area.

Understanding On Floor Information

As with LDB, OFI is available only for CBOT contracts. We are currently working with other exchanges to make this information available for their exchange-traded products.

How are the numbers calculated? At the end of the day, a special file is created by the CBOT Clearing Corporation with a breakdown of filled orders generated from off the floor. From this information, we calculate the average size of the buy order and the average size of the sell order. The average size of the buy order divided by the average size of the sell order yields the OFI number.

Some hypothetical numbers generated for the 10-year note will serve as an example. Assume that on the day, 2000 sell tickets generated from off the floor were filled. Second, assume those 2000 sell orders constituted 30,000 contracts. The 30,000 contracts divided by the 2000 filled orders yield an average sell ticket of 15 contracts. The same information generated from the other side of the ledger yields the average size of the buy ticket. Assume that there were only 1000 filled tickets generated from off the floor on the buy side. Also assume that those 1000 buy orders encompassed 20,000 contracts. The 20,000 contracts divided by the 1000 filled orders give an average buy ticket of 20 contracts. Lastly, divide the average size of the buy ticket by the average size of the sell ticket. For this example, the average size of the buy ticket of 20 contracts divided by the average size of the sell ticket of 15 contracts gives an OFI ratio of 1.33.

In looking at this example, a couple questions may be raised. Why were the contracts traded on the buy side and the sell side not equal? Why were the number of filled tickets not equal? The only place things need to balance is at the clearinghouse; at that point there needs to be a buy contract for every sell contract. This function can be accomplished by crossing orders in a specialist's book, trades being crossed from off the floor participants, or having a local take the other side of a trade. In stocks, they may delay the opening of a stock because of an order imbalance. The same underlying phenomenon can exist with commodities. An example would be when the clear majority of outside orders entering the pit were on the sell side. In this case, the local gets buried because the day is trending lower and she or he is constantly fading the flows. An extreme example of one-sided order flow would be limit activity.

Looking back at the example, the OFI ratio is 1.33. What does this mean? From an absolute sense, it means that the average size of the filled buy ticket was 1.33 times greater than the average size of the filled sell ticket. If the OFI number is greater than 1.0, then the average filled buy ticket is greater than the average filled sell ticket. This is called OFI buying. In the example, if the number of contracts traded and the number of filled orders were switched from buy to sell and sell to buy, an average size buy ticket of 15 contracts and an average size sell ticket of 20 contracts would result. To get the OFI ratio, buys (15) are divided by sells (20) to get an OFI ratio of 0.75. When the OFI number is less than 1.0, the average size of the filled sell ticket is greater than the average size of the filled buy ticket. This is OFI selling. When the OFI number is 1.0, then the average size of the buy ticket and the average size of the sell ticket are pretty much equal.

For a visual, the OFI buying (>1.0) is placed below the profile for that day. When OFI selling (<1.0) occurs, the ratio is placed above the profile for that day. Once again, what I am trying to convey to the reader is how the big guy is positioned. When trading, one typically wants to be following the lead of the big trader, not the odd-lot guy. In stocks, one would like to be positioned like Peter Lynch or Warren Buffet. In commodities, position oneself with the likes of George Soros or Paul Tudor Jones. The reason is that these guys know their business and can defend their positions. From a macro perspective, Warren Buffet may buy GM stock at 51 and more at 48 because he believes his idea will win out in the end; therefore, he will defend his position. We are trying to convey the same information with OFI. How the big guy is positioned. Knowing how the big guy acts is an edge. This information is generated after the close so it can be used for the next day's trade (or during the night session for those contracts traded 24 hours). When the numbers are skewed (this varies depending on the commodity one is trading), the big barn boss can be expected to defend his position for the first quarter of the trading session. Thus, one wants to be trading with a like bias out of the box.

Figure 7–2 is the standard OFI display generated from Capflow32—the Market Profile graphic with a number affixed to the top or bottom of each profile. Any OFI numbers equal to or greater than 1.00 are at the bottom of the profile, indicating OFI buying. Any OFI number less than 1.00 is displayed above the daily profile, indicating OFI selling. In Figure 7–2, the first pro-

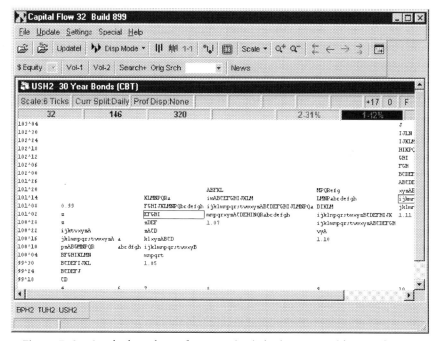

Figure 7–2   Standard On Floor Information (OFI) display generated from Capflow32.
Copyright © 1984 Chicago Board of Trade. All Rights Reserved. CBOT Market Profile, Market Profile, Liquidity Data Bank, and LDB are registered trademarks of the Chicago Board of Trade. All Rights Reserved. Provided by Steidlmayer Software Inc.

file in the display has a number of 0.99 above the profile, indicating OFI selling. The rest of the profiles have their numbers below the profiles, indicating OFI buying. The numbers below the profiles chronologically are 1.05, 1.07, 1.10, and 1.11. This means that the average size of the buy ticket filled from off the floor versus the average size of the sell ticket filled from off the floor is getting proportionally larger for the buy side.

To help you appreciate the value of this type of information, I include one more OFI printout and the corresponding daily bar chart. Figure 7–3 is an OFI screen display of the 30-year Treasury bond. The three profiles on the right of the screen have OFI numbers displayed. The numbers are 0.87, 1.02, and 0.86 from left to right for the three profiles. Recall that OFI numbers equal to or greater than 1.0 indicate buying,

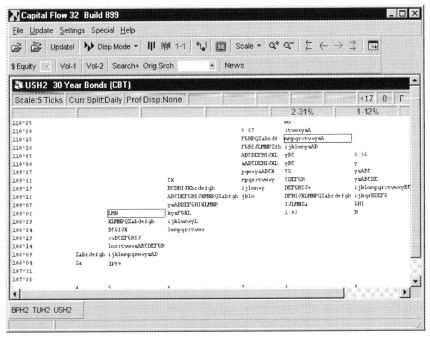

Figure 7–3   OFI screen display of the 30-year Treasury bond.

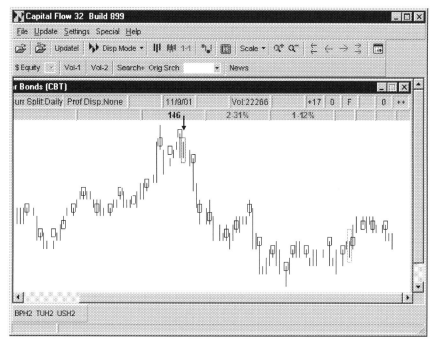

Figure 7–4   Daily bar chart of the 30-year Treasury bond with most recent OFI selling day denoted by down arrow.

Provided by Steidlmayer Software Inc.

and OFI numbers less than 1.0 indicate selling. Additionally, the farther the OFI number is from 1.0 to the upside or downside, the stronger the off floor buying or selling activity. Looking at these three consecutive numbers shows the two selling OFI numbers (0.87 and 0.86) are way below 1.0, whereas 1.02 is only 0.02 percent above 1.0. In other words, the big-ticket sell orders coming from off the floor are much larger proportionally than the big-ticket buy orders. Figure 7–4 is a daily bar chart of the 30-year Treasury bond with the last of the three OFI numbers (0.86) from Figure 7–3 denoted by the arrow. Note how prices eroded lower following the OFI setup. The big barn boss had the market on the ropes, and once things started going his way, he was able to really push the envelope.

Understanding Volume @ Time

When looking at volume, the most forward-looking and revolutionary tool for Market Profile users is volume @ time. Steidlmayer Software developed this application in 1998 and it was integrated into Capflow32.

We took the online volume from stock exchanges, electronic future exchanges, and open outcry exchanges (when available) and integrated it into the Market Profile. This allows for the creation of an entirely new database, a volume database. Now people can trade a price database (Market Profile), a volume database, or a combination of the two.

How does it work? The price and volume information is recorded as it accumulates over time. Look at the industry standard Market Profile, which is half-hour data, and record the volume and price range for each half-hour segment. Compare that half-hour's range (the existing) to the previous and determine whether it rotated up (took out the high of the previous half-hour but not the low), rotated down (took out the previous half-hour's low but not the high), was an inside half-hour (did not talk out the previous half-hour's high or low), or was an outside half-hour (took out the previous half-hour's high and low). Volume @ time analysis throws out the volume information for inside and outside half-hours. Volume for inside and outside half-hour bars is not calculated because direction is not assignable. It defines a half-hour rotation up as money flow into the stock or commodity, and a half-hour rotation down as money flow out of the stock or commodity. Thus, from a daily Market Profile perspective, one can look at all the half-hour rotations up/down with their corresponding volume and define a net money flow for the defined unit.

Figure 7–5 is a printout of the volume @ time information generated from Capflow32. In the upper left hand corner of the spreadsheet is the name of the underlying (in this case CAT, Caterpillar stock). In this printout, focus on the column heading Vol($), which gives us volume dollars over the past 22 units (each line bottom to top represents a profile 22 units back to the most recent).

Finally, one has an objective tool to measure money flow. Previously, one needed to make a subjective assessment of the

Equity $	Vol($)	Slider
-14	0	588	-181
172	0	1318	
		1312	
243	0	694	
90	0	383	
22	0	484	
81	0	607	
175	0	618	
132	0	565	
102	0	522	
56	0	353	
		262	
		114	
		-101	
		-270	
		-604	
		-120	
		-155	
		-81	
		-112	
		160	
		141	

Figure 7–5   Caterpillar (CAT), Equity/Volume $ comparison grid.
Provided by Steidlmayer Software Inc.

market (is the market trying to move higher or lower?). Knowing the volume representative of that unit, one would anticipate continuation or change. As a side note, we know we are measuring the market correctly with volume @ time because on average at the end of the day, when there is positive net money flow, the price is higher than the previous day, and when there is negative net money flow the price is lower than the previous day.

Figures 7–6 and 7–7 show two more printouts of volume @ time output. Figure 7–6 is a printout of Sears (S). In the column with the heading Vol($), one sees that toward the bottom of the printout (farthest back in time) is a mixture of positive and negative numbers, then the 15 most recent entries are positive. In other words, there was a little chop of money flowing into and out of Sears stock until the buying really took hold.

Figure 7–7 paints a completely different picture. The printout is for the stock Global Crossings (GBLX). Starting at the bottom of the printout all the way to the top are all negative num-

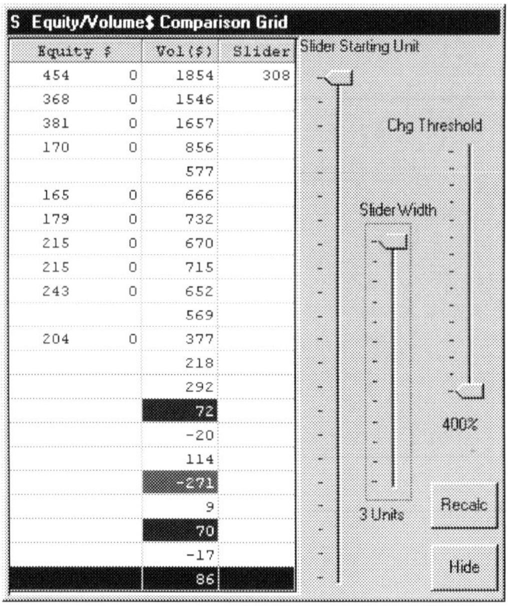

Equity $		Vol($)	Slider
454	0	1854	308
368	0	1546	
381	0	1657	
170	0	856	
		577	
165	0	666	
179	0	732	
215	0	670	
215	0	715	
243	0	652	
		569	
204	0	377	
		218	
		292	
		72	
		-20	
		114	
		-271	
		9	
		70	
		-17	
		86	

Figure 7–6 Sears Equity/Volume $ comparison grid.
Provided by Steidlmayer Software Inc.

bers. There are points in time where the numbers in the Vol($) column do become less negative than the previous unit (indicating some buying coming into the stock); however, there is never a point in time over the 22-unit sample at which net buying dollars for the stock turns positive (numbers > 0). In fact, the unit at the bottom of the printout, which is the farthest back in time, has the least negative number (−403), and the unit at the top of the printout, which represents the most recent unit, has the most negative value (−3894) over the 22-unit sample. One would have to conclude that the money flow is trending down or out of Global Crossings over the referenced segment of time.

Steps in Interpreting the Liquidity Data Bank Report

The primary purpose of the LDB report is to help determine the likelihood of *continuation* or *change* in the market. The steps to help make this determination are:

1. Try to determine what direction the market was trying to go during the session. Was it trying to go higher, lower, a mixture of both—or is it impossible to tell? Do not be embarrassed to put a question mark here—sometimes it is difficult to determine.

2. Having made this determination to the best of one's ability, check whether volume was higher or lower than the previous day. In general more volume, coupled with a clear direction for the market, means continuation; lower volume means change.

3. Compare the range of the volume value area for the day to that of the previous day. Is it larger or smaller? If it is larger and the market is up, it is a positive sign for continuation; if it is smaller, it is a negative sign for continuation in that direction.

In trying to determine whether to anticipate higher, lower, or unchanged values, one must weigh the variables as opposed to just adding up the pluses and the minuses. Learn to select and focus

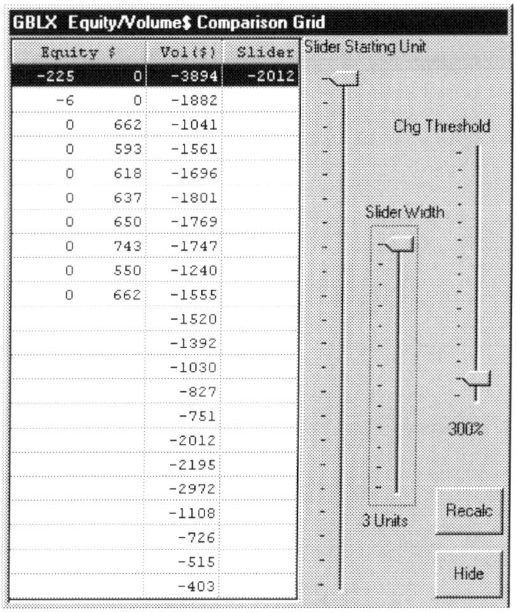

Figure 7–7   Global Crossings Equity/Volume $ comparison grid.
Provided by Steidlmayer Software Inc.

on the most important factor. This will vary from time to time. But generally the most important variable is trade facilitation direction. Simply stated, trade facilitation direction is nothing more than the directional price movement confirmed by volume. The second most important piece of information is whether volume is higher or lower; the third most important is the range of the volume value area. Lastly, when commercial activity is abnormal—not selling high or buying low or funds are active buying high or selling low—this may be the most important factor in the market because it may signal a bigger change.

Figure 7–8, which is an LDB printout of the 30-year Treasury bonds, helps illustrate a point. On a daily basis, commercials are active participants buying what they perceive to be the low end of value and selling what they perceive to be the upper end of value. They need to do this to facilitate their day-to-day operations. At times, they are very accurate in picking these boundaries; at other times, they are less accurate. In general, they do have a degree of participation at these levels that is measurable. One does not want to focus on what is standard or normal, but instead on what is abnormal. One wants to isolate instances when they are unusually active at an extreme, signaling some form of commercial capping. Figure 7–8 is such an example. Recall that commercials have the CTI code of CTI-2. Under the CTI-2 column, I have shaded the corresponding five rows at the top and five rows at the bottom of the LDB printout with their corresponding percent of volume breakdown numbers. I have also shaded the total volume for each of the five prices at the top of the profile and the five prices at the bottom of the profile. Some simple multiplication and addition will determine the commercial activity at the extremes. Take the total volume at each of the five prices at the highs and multiply by the corresponding commercial activity percentage to come up with commercial activity at each price and then with a total for the five high prices. Do the same thing for the five prices at the bottom of the printout. One is now able to compare the commercial activity at the high with the commercial activity at the low. One is also able to see how today's commercial activity at the extremes compared with some norm. In our example, if the numbers are crunched, the commercial volume at the top totaled

```
CHICAGO BOARD OF TRADE                          LIQUIDITY DATA BANK* REPORT

                    VOLUME/FUTURES SUMMARY REPORT FOR 01 14 02

COMMODITY  --  T-BOND (CBOT) DAY       MAR 02


Volume Summary
```

Price	Volume	%Vol	%Cti1	%Cti2	%Cti3	%Cti4	Brackets
10400	12	0.0	50.0	0.0	0.0	25.0	A
10331	3554	2.5	60.6	3.0	2.3	34.2	ABEG
10330	7042	5.0	55.4	4.7	6.0	33.9	ABDEG
10329	8538	6.0	56.9	9.9	7.3	26.0	ABCDEFGH
10328	12398	8.8	55.8	5.0	4.1	35.0	ABCDEFGH
10327	11740	8.3	57.1	9.5	6.3	27.1	$ABCDEFGHI
10326	17784	12.6	50.7	3.7	4.5	41.2	$ABCDEFGHI
10325	8328	5.9	58.7	5.7	7.5	28.0	$ABCDEFHI
10324	10032	7.1	59.1	5.2	6.8	28.9	$ABCDEFI
10323	6638	4.7	64.4	6.5	8.1	21.0	$ABCEFI
10322	11072	7.8	56.2	3.7	6.5	33.6	$ABCEFIJ
10321	4904	3.5	66.9	5.3	5.5	22.3	$ABCEFIJ
10320	2616	1.9	62.0	1.6	8.9	27.5	Z$CIJ
10319	4254	3.0	61.1	2.9	9.1	26.8	Z$CIJ
10318	2706	1.9	65.8	4.2	9.3	20.6	ZCIJ
10317	3834	2.7	59.8	3.6	7.7	28.8	ZIJ
10316	3210	2.3	57.9	3.5	8.0	30.6	ZJK
10315	2322	1.6	58.2	0.1	5.0	36.6	ZJK
10314	2868	2.0	64.8	0.0	6.5	28.7	JKL
10313	3262	2.3	65.4	0.4	4.3	30.0	JKL
10312	6396	4.5	52.2	11.0	6.1	30.6	KL
10311	2712	1.9	61.5	2.8	7.1	28.6	KLM
10310	1566	1.1	55.0	1.1	3.3	40.5	KLM
10309	3090	2.2	58.3	15.8	8.1	17.9	LM
10308	510	0.4	50.6	0.0	0.6	48.6	LM

```
70%   10330   101092  71.5  57.0   5.6   6.1   31.3 Z$ABCDEFGHIJ
V-A   10320
```

Figure 7–8   LDB Report, T-Bond.

1906 contracts and the commercial activity at the bottom totaled 1300. Relative to the current unit, the selling activity
amounted to almost 150 percent of the buying commercial participation. But more importantly, the 1906 contracts sold over
the five highest ticks of the day would be categorized as unusually heavy commercial participation.

   So what effect did this commercial capping have on subsequent price activity? Look at a daily bar chart of the 30-year
Treasury bond to see. Figure 7–9 is a daily bar chart of the bonds

with the LDB printout date highlighted by a down arrow and a heavily shaded vertical line running from the top to bottom of that days price range. One can see from the bar chart that on the 2 days following the commercial capping day, the market did trade marginally higher, only to see a swift three-point break. This commercial capping area is a "zone of prices," which the commercial perceives as being away from value. It may take other participants longer to come to this realization. Commercials will always be present throughout the day's range; it is important to recognize when they are acting outside their normal participation levels.

One can do the same type of analysis for fund activity. Funds fall under CTI-4. Funds typically play go-with and commercials play fade. Therefore, one would expect to see the opposite type of subsequent price activity following extremely high volume under CTI-4 (funds). Abnormally high volume by funds would

Figure 7–9   Daily bar chart of the 30-year Treasury bond with day of heavy commercial selling denoted by down arrow.

Provided by CQG.

signal continuation (follow through) because funds typically sell low and buy high, looking for follow through.

Steps in Interpreting On Floor Information

As stated earlier, OFI will give traders a handle on how the big guys are positioned in the market. In trading, one wants to be positioned with one's back to the wall, eliminating one side of the market. One wants to be able to scratch the trade or make money. One wants to avoid markets when they are in a state of pure random activity and participate when they are nonrandom. One wants to find an edge.

OFI can be used to indicate when markets are in that nonrandom state. This nonrandom state could be short-lived or more of a longer-term phenomenon, depending on how actively the big barn boss wants to defend his position and the number of additional participants playing the market from a like perspective.

When looking at the OFI numbers, every market has a standard that should be used to indicate a random versus a nonrandom environment. When generating a number at or beyond this threshold indicating participation by the "big barn boss," the life of that participant should be (barring any economic numbers, political events, etc.) at least the first hour and a half of the next day's trade. Beyond that first hour and a half, all bets are off because new participants with a new perspective can overwhelm the previous day's idea.

Look at Figure 7–10 to help illustrate how to interpret and trade the OFI numbers. This is the March 5-year note contract that is traded on the CBOT. The lowercase letters in the profiles reference the nonparallel trading session and the uppercase letters reference the side-by-side session or when there is floor trade. The OFI numbers are generated by floor trade only. Looking at the five profiles displayed in Figure 7–10, one sees that the second profile from the left has OFI buying (number > 1.0 and positioned below the profile) and the remainder of the profiles have OFI selling (number < 1.0 and positioned above the profile). Once again, this information should be traded to go with the

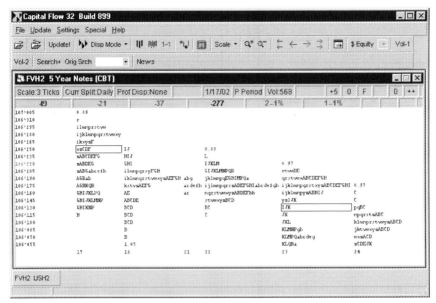

Figure 7–10   Five-year note contract with OFI numbers affixed to profiles.

Copyright © 1984 Chicago Board of Trade. All Rights Reserved. CBOT Market Profile, Market Profile, Liquidity Data Bank, and LDB are registered trademarks of the Chicago Board of Trade. All Rights Reserved. Provided by Steidlmayer Software Inc.

large-order flow for the first hour and a half of the day following the day the information is generated. The only buying OFI day was March 18, so one would be playing the market from the long side the following day, March 22. On that day, the market opened lower and was able to grind higher for the rest of the day. When we received the OFI information on the evening of March 22, we had OFI selling (number < 1.0 and positioned above profile) so we would be playing the next day (March 23) from the short side. Lo and behold, the market opened unchanged to lower on March 23 and had a significant sell off. In fact, every day in this sequence would have worked out well.

Steps in Interpreting Volume @ Time

Volume @ time allows for the creation of an entirely new database for profile users. To date, this volume database is available only in Steidlmayer Software's Capflow32 (other data providers will make this information available in 2002). A great deal of flexibility has been built into this program. The user can create a faster or slower database based on preferences. Additionally, one can call up displays that crunch data differently to get different output.

When using volume @ time, one can apply standard volume interpretations to this unique way of measuring volume or apply some of our proprietary methods. By standard volume analysis, I mean increased volume signaling continuation and decreased volume signaling change. Another standard volume application for Market Profile users is size of the value area, which usually has a positive correlation to the day's range. In general, larger value areas signal continuation and smaller value areas signal stopping or change.

Moving beyond standard volume analysis, there are some powerful tools internal to the volume @ time program that can be used to measure the market objectively. The output measurement of volume @ time is volume dollars, whose calculation was discussed earlier in this chapter. By "netting" out the volume information in a block of data (profile), one is able to determine whether money is flowing into or out of the given instrument at that moment in time.

Volume @ time generates an array of information that can be combined to formulate a multitude of outputs. At this time, we focus on the three most objective outputs: blow off extreme, volume excess, and zero line.

Blow Off Extreme

Conceptually, what we are trying to do is find that point in time at which many of the participants are on the wrong side of the market and falling all over each other trying to get out. The footprint of this phenomenon is heavy volume and exhaustive price movement. The backdrop for something like this would be a consensus of activity against some perceived support or resistance level that does not hold. Trading through these levels opens the floodgates of anxiety and panic. When the dust finally settles, the consensus participant has exited his or her position at a disadvantageous price only to see the market ultimately unfold as expected. In their haste to get out at all costs, the masses have created a price probe on heavy volume that took out the top or bottom of some development area and then reentered that preexisting development area. This is called the blow off extreme, the price spike on heavy volume. Trade the low of this unit against the bottom of some consolidation area or the top of this unit against the top of some consolidation area with the expectation of it serving as an extreme for some time to come.

Within the universe of Capflow32 users, it will be denoted as a red profile when called up under the capital flow profile display. Figure 7–11 denotes such an extreme in the stock Gillette. Lacking color examples, we have placed a box around the profile

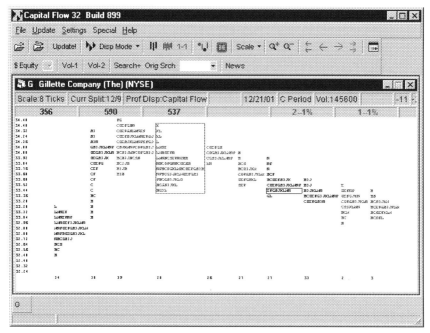

Figure 7–11   Gillette Company with box around profile referencing volume spike. Copyright © 1984 Chicago Board of Trade. All Rights Reserved. CBOT Market Profile, Market Profile, Liquidity Data Bank, and LDB are registered trademarks of the Chicago Board of Trade. All Rights Reserved. Provided by Steidlmayer Software Inc.

that would appear as solid red. Once this volume profile spikes toward any extreme of development, one puts on a position buying against the bottom of development or selling (in the case of Gillette) against the top of development with a protective stop through the high of the unit with the volume spike (red profile). Referring back to Figure 7–11, the high of the unit with the box around it is 34.50. Realizing that we would not be able to initiate a short position until the unit with the box around it is complete, we would need to initiate our short in the price range of the profile one unit to the right of the unit with the box around it. Typically I look to initiate positions halfway back into the volume spike, ($34.00) with a protective stop above the high of the box at 34.60. Over the next 30 trading days, Gillette never traded above 34.00 and managed to trade down to 31.50, an 8 percent break from where the stock was shorted. Those not having access to Capflow32 can use standard volume information and look for the volume spike against some consolidation area and trade against that volume spike.

Volume Excess

The next type of output to consider is volume excess. The trader's approach to this phenomenon is similar to the blow off extreme (buy low, sell high); however, the output is generated in a different manner. Conceptually, we are finding situations where there is directional integrity (string of money flow numbers getting more positive or more negative) and finding that change point that reverses the direction. This change point will serve as the reference point to trade against. What needs to be emphasized here is that the change point and reference units (all of which are profiles) are not price points but volume$ calculations (explained at the beginning of this chapter). We are totally discounting price and making volume$ our sole information source and trade trigger. Management of the trade is also from a volume$ perspective, not price.

How can I trade this concept? All volume @ time analysis can be generated with Capflow32; thus, any Capflow32 user will have this information at her or his fingertips. Those interested in this product can contact the coauthor Steve Hawkins at his website (steve@profiletrading.com) and he will be able to answer any of your questions. For this volume excess study, there is an automated read function built into the program that highlighted the most recent excess unit as one moves the cursor over the individual profiles. As the cursor is moved over the excess unit, the dollar value of the excess unit is highlighted in green in the reference area of the screen display.

For those more comfortable with spreadsheet displays, there is a volume$ display sheet that can be used to generate the same information, find the excess. In the center column under the heading volume$ are the calculations for the most recent 22 units (profiles). At the top of the spreadsheet is the current profile information, moving from top to bottom one goes from current to current minus 22 units. Another interesting piece of information displayed on the Equity/Volume$ Comparison Grid is Equity $ column (left-most column). What this tells is the profit and loss generated from the coding of Market Profiles. What we are attempting to do here is objectify the information generated from a Market Profile display and hard-code this criterion to give a directional bias in the form of a directional arrow. This information is then displayed in the left-most column over the past 10 units based on being long or short the selected stock or commodity. In other words, it indicates how much one is up or down being long or short this contract. To determine profit and loss based upon the arrows, look at the left-most column, Equity $. Each row has two numbers, one of which is zero. Focus on the number that is not a zero to find out how much you have made (if number is positive) or lost (if number is negative). To determine whether the most recent directional arrow is buying or selling, bisect the Equity $ column down the middle; if the nonzero number in the row is on the left side, the directional arrow is buying, and if the nonzero number is on the right side, the directional arrow is signaling selling. Thus, this spreadsheet brings together a price database output and a volume database output.

Looking for the excess in the spreadsheet is straightforward. If one is looking for an excess over the most recent 22 units (maximum allowable within software), one looks for the most positive number or most negative number over the data set. Look at the stock Mattel Inc. (MAT) for our example. The most positive number on the spreadsheet happens to be 64 volume$. The representative unit is one row up from the bottom of the spreadsheet (Figure 7–12). The number in the boxes adjacent to this number is −29 below and −320 above. Knowing that one moves back in time as one moves from the top of the spreadsheet to the bottom, one realizes −320 is the most recent of the three, 64 the middle unit, and −29 the oldest unit of the three. A graph of this would look something like a head and shoulders formation with a lower right shoulder. In other words, money was flowing into the stock (from −29 to 64), where it peaked out and money then flowed out of the stock to where volume dollars amounted to −320. This configuration sets up our excess—we know 64 is the excess because the right shoulder is lower (−320) than the left shoulder (−29) signaling a price high and loss of momentum (most recent shoulder is lower than oldest shoulder).

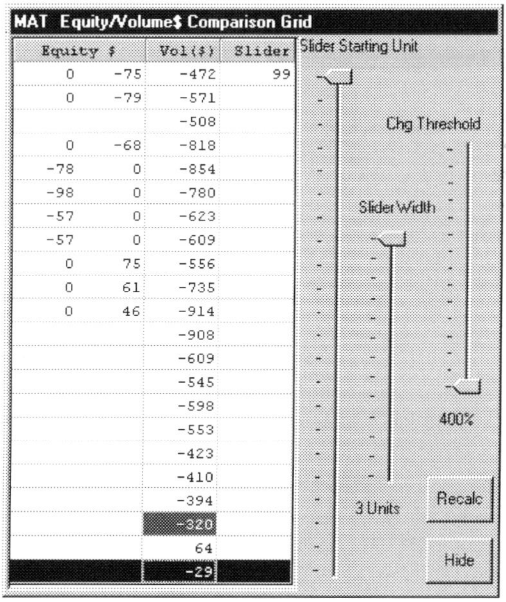

Figure 7–12   Mattel Inc. with Equity/Volume $ Comparison Grid.
Provided by Steidlmayer Software Inc.

To get a price perspective of how this money flow example un-folded, look at Figure 7–13, which is a segmented market activity display of Mattel. Count back 21 units (balls and lines) from the right-hand side of the screen to find the starting point for the vol-ume$ analysis. An arrow along with a large rectangular box is drawn around the ball that references the excess (64 volume$ on spreadsheet printout). Looking at the chart, one sees that prices have eroded lower relative to price just as they have with volume$.

The inverse of this setup is seen with Novellus Systems (NVLS) with a volume excess to the downside. Finding the least positive or most negative number would cause one to look at the volume numbers adjacent to this potential excess. In this exam-ple, the most negative number is −60 (in fact it is the only neg-

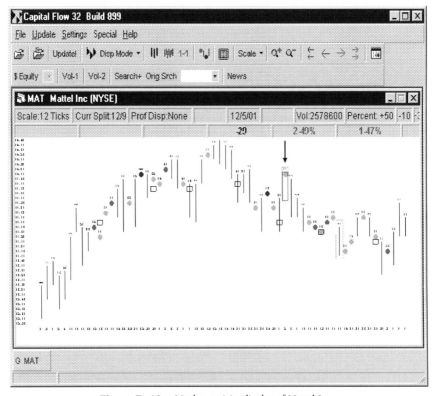

Figure 7–13   Market activity display of Mattel Inc.

Provided by Steidlmayer Software Inc.

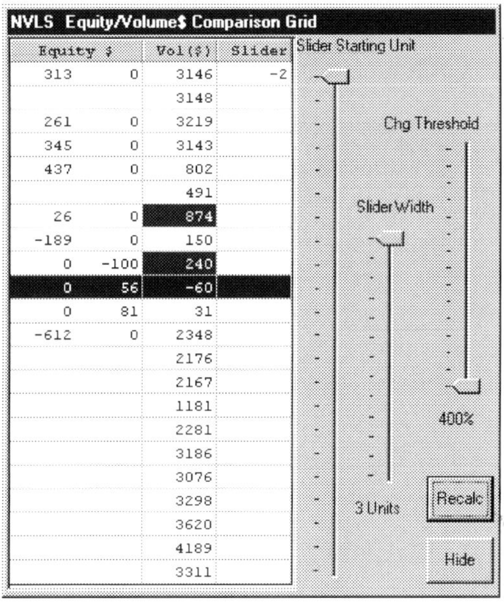

NVLS Equity/Volume$ Comparison Grid

Equity $	Vol($)	Slider
313	0	3146
		3148
261	0	3219
345	0	3143
437	0	802
		491
26	0	874
-189	0	150
0	-100	240
0	56	-60
0	81	31
-612	0	2348
		2176
		2167
		1181
		2281
		3186
		3076
		3298
		3620
		4189
		3311

Slider panel: Slider Starting Unit — Chg Threshold — Slider Width — 400% — 3 Units — Recalc — Hide

Figure 7–14   Novellus Systems with volume $ excess highlighted.
Provided by Steidlmayer Software Inc.

ative number in this spreadsheet). This row is shaded in Figure 7–14 and one can see the number above to be 240 and the number below to be 31—our setup for an excess is in place. Graphically, this would appear as an inverted head and shoulders with a higher right shoulder: the left shoulder being 31, the head being −60, and the right shoulder being 240. With the excess in place, one enters the trade managing it from a volume perspective, not price. One does not exit on adverse price movement, one trades volume$ and if the volume$ excess amount is taken out, one exits the trade because conditions have changed. Figure 7–15 can be used to locate the volume$ excess in a chart display. Our volume excess number (−60) is 10 lines down from the top of the screen, therefore, we need to count back 10 units from the right-hand side of the screen to find the corresponding volume$ excess on the bar chart. A box has been drawn around the volume$ excess unit. On our market activity display notice how this excess level was the trough from which the market rallied.

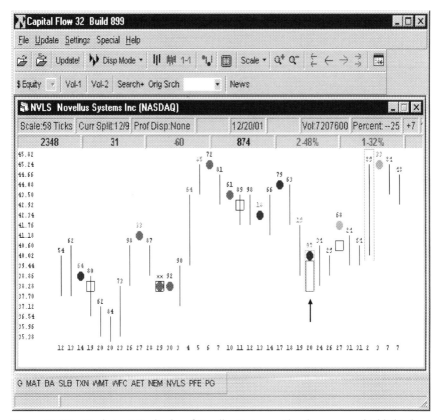

Figure 7–15   Market activity display of Novellus Systems with volume excess highlighted with up arrow.
Provided by Steidlmayer Software Inc.

For those who do not subscribe to Steidlmayer Software's Capflow32, the volume excess concept can still be applied to any market that has online volume readily available. Whether one is looking at a resolution of 5-minutes, 30-minutes, hourly, or daily, the volume excess should be a valuable indicator. In addition, other vendors will be providing this platform by the time this book is published. Contact Steve@profiletrading.com for information.

Zero Line

The zero line is a display that can overlay a bar chart that uses a histogram format to display volume$ for the most recent 22 units. If the individual unit has positive volume$, a proportional histogram will appear above the horizontal zero line; if the unit has negative volume$, a proportional histogram bar will appear below the horizontal zero line. Thus, the name zero line. This display reinforces our theory on the one-dimensionality of markets that states markets feature a preponderance of buying or selling, not random buying and selling. When one calls up a stock or commodity with this display, one usually does not get more than one change (histogram moving from above to below zero line or from below to above zero line for any duration); if more than one change occurs, it signals randomness—stay away from that market. Use the zero line as a bias indicator (if the most recent histogram is above the zero line, be long; if the most recent histogram bar is below the zero line, be short). Using the analogy of rolling a boulder up a hill is a good visual to convey how to trigger a trade. When the market is in a selling mode

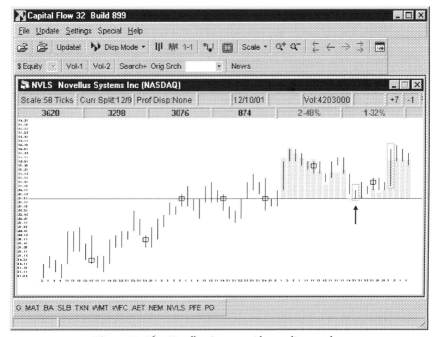

Figure 7–16   Novellus Systems with zero line overlay.
Provided by Steidlmayer Software Inc.

(string of histogram bars below the zero line), wave after wave of buying must enter the market to bring the market toward balance (back to zero line). At which point, the buying has run its course and selling can reenter the market and prices will erode lower. Push and push and push the boulder until all your energy has been expelled only to lose control of the boulder and watch it roll back down to the bottom of the hill. The inverse should hold true when the bias indicator (zero line) signals be long. In the Novellus example, selling enters the market under a positive volume$ scenario (all histogram bars are above zero line), only to exhaust itself and allow for a further rally (Fig. 7–16). Counting back 10 bars from the right-hand side of the screen, one finds one unit over the past 22 units that is below the zero line (indicated by the up arrow). At this moment, the money flow is −60 and volume$ grows after that.

That concludes the chapter on volume analysis. What one needs to do as a profile user is integrate relevant information into the analysis whenever it becomes available. Technology and the concept of measuring volume @ time necessitate change from old to new. Change for the sake of change is not necessarily good; however, change that advances a society, an industry, a theory, or an individual is good. Seize the opportunity to advance your program.

Chapter 8

THE STEIDLMAYER THEORY
OF MARKETS

A theory must be practical and capable of being used by people, otherwise it is of little value. Throughout this book, I have tried to combine practical guidelines for learning how to read and use the markets with the underlying principles of how markets work. This chapter discusses in concise form the theory of markets that has grown out of our work. The meaning and practical implications of each phrase in the theory are explained in some detail. By the end of this discussion, the reader should have all the basic information needed to understand markets and how they work. The Steidlmayer theory of markets is that the market is a organized medium that expresses human behaviors in different price areas at a given point in time, always presenting an opportunity to someone. Though this statement appears simple, it contains a lot of meaning. Look closely at each word to fully understand the theory and its implications for a trader.

The Market . . .

The market is a location that constitutes a base for services. It establishes rules and regulations for participants and products and a centralized meeting place in which market activity takes place. In the past, market locations have been fixed in major centers around the world, known as exchanges. With the advent of changes in communications and the globalization of markets, these fixed locations are now subject to change in terms of the new services that the market place now requires. The first service the market provides is liquidity, which allows transactions to take place in an orderly fashion. The orderly nature of market transactions makes it possible for market participants to read market activity, which, in turn, leads to the single most important service provided by the market: information. Information on transactions is vital to all traders and needs to be disseminated on an on-line, real-time basis so that market activity can be defined with volume. Three elements are necessary in a complete market information source: price, time, and volume. These should be provided in a flexible format, as they have occurred and are occurring in the marketplace. As this information is disseminated to more people, the markets tend to expand, serving the industry in a better, broader fashion.

Is an Organized Medium . . .

The most revealing aspect of the market is the fact that it is naturally organized, not chaotic (as it appears on the surface). The key to this organization is the negotiation process used by market participants. What takes place in the negotiation process is the development of three reference points: the trade price at which trade is consummated, and reference points above and below the trade price. The reference point above the trade price is apparently too high; the reference point below the trade price is apparently too low. In a more complex negotiation process, another structure that gives further organization is the auction process. In this situation, instead of a single buyer and seller, there are multiple participants who would like to buy or sell. This is also a known procedure for finding a single buyer and seller in a competitive format. In the auction process, if 10 people are interested in buying at a certain price, as the price moves higher, participants drop out. For example, if an item is priced at $10 with 10 buyers interested, if the price moves to $15, 6 buyers may be interested; if the price moves to $20, we may have 2 buyers interested; and so on, until the transaction is finally consummated. Two types of auctions take place that may be confusing to the uninitiated: the down auction, in which multiple participants wish to sell, and the up auction, in which multiple participants wish to buy. In either case, the market is ordered around the fact that as price moves, it rations the activity of people wishing to buy or sell. Buying or selling activity is shut off as the price moves higher or lower.

That Expresses Human Behavior . . .

This refers to the use of the market by participants. Market development, which is the continual use of the market during its trading hours, consists of six things: a current price, a reference price that is too low, a reference price that is too high, a price area that is recurring, any change in any of these, and the relationship of each element to the others. From a small cell, not unlike John Schultz's minimum trend, the unit that includes each of these six elements will evolve from relative instability at a small sample size to relative stability as the market develops. That is, the reference points become more stable and reliable as the process continues. The weakness of past market theories, and the reason they have been largely impractical, is their failure to consider human behavior. The most important point past market theories have missed is that human behavior is never balanced. Because human behavior is so, opportunities can be defined in any market place. Individuals and corporations in industries outside the financial community do this every day; yet amazingly this basic concept has never been applied to exchange markets. In essence, human behavior in the market is price/time allocation, which is affected by each of four major kinds of group activity: confident activity, hesitant activity, gradual change, and beginning and ending activity occurring simultaneously in the same price area. There are also three main groups of market participants, each of which affects human activity in the marketplace in a different way: the local/specialist, the commercials/institution, and the general market participants. These groups are discussed in detail elsewhere in this book.

In Different Price Areas at a Given Point in Time . . .

Different price areas refers to the vertical range of prices in which all market activity takes place. The range of this distribution is important, and it gives the market a time parameter. The relationship can be defined in this way: the larger the range, the longer the market will remain in that price area because it will take the market longer to unwind. By the same token, a small distribution gives one a small amount of time because the market can unwind more quickly. Two other components that add to the stability of a distribution are the diversification of participants and the amount of trading volume. For instance, if there is a large distribution with a diversified clientele of market participants, then the market is probably in a rather stable condition. However, unstable conditions can arise if the large, diversified clientele was operating from a single motive; when this motive disappears, the market may unwind very quickly. A good example occurred during the October/November timeframe of 2001 in the 10-year and 30-year interest rate contracts at the Chicago Board of Trade (CBOT). Falling interest rates caused Fannie Mae (FNMA), Ginnie Mae (GNMA) and similar classes of participants to buy futures contracts in anticipation of mortgage redemptions. This convexity buying or duration shortening fueled more buying. When the motive disappeared, selling ensued in the futures that in turn fed on itself because higher rates meant fewer redemptions. By the same token, if the diversified clientele is replaced by a single operator causing a large price range on big volume, the stability of the market may again be weakened. In our analysis of the market, we are dealing with the present tense conditions that exist and are evolving now. Our on-line database gives us price information from the past up to the present, defining the current point in time and any changes taking place in it.

Always Presenting an Opportunity to Someone

There are three time frames in any marketplace: the market-imposed time frame, defined by the operating hours of the exchange; the participant time frame, which is the individual trader's time frame for buying or selling; and the opportunity time frame. The opportunity time frame is a moment in the market that forces a participant to act because of the favorable price opportunity it offers. In the past, there were two main types of traders: day time frame traders and beyond-the-day traders. Day time frame traders are simply looking for a fair price. Those who trade beyond the day are more distant from the market; they are not interested in trading unless a very favorable opportunity is presented. As the markets move toward 24-hour trading, the first two time frames are taking a smaller role, and the opportunity time frame trader is growing in importance. Today's opportunity time frame trader is distinguished from the beyond-the-day trader by the fact that the opportunity trader must watch the markets closely and continually, to ferret out the opportunity that may arise at any time. So he or she is closer to the market and follows it rigorously, knowing that he or she may want to trade at any time of the day or night—whenever a trading opportunity may arise. The emergence of this new type of trader is contributing to the volatility of today's markets. He or she generally follows one of two behavior patterns: if the market gets too far away, he or she may conclude that there will be an opportunity to do just as well a day or 2 down the road, and so he or she will wait patiently; or, if he or she has just missed the best price opportunity by a small margin, he or she may follow the market and trade at a price away from the best opportunity. The purpose of the market is to serve society by bringing more people into the distribution system. Thus, it is important for the market to increasingly attract participants who are already active in the market (increasing the use of the market place) as well as attract new participants from the outside. The Steidlmayer theory of markets draws together, in a simple form, many of the conclusions reached as a result of years of practical work in various markets. We think the reader will find it a useful framework within which to organize thinking about markets and how they work. Trading practices that are based on a sound understanding of market activity are likely to succeed; those that are not soundly based may work for a time, but, as markets change, they will no longer apply. Without a fundamental market understanding, one will lack a solid foundation from which to make the necessary adjustments. Thus, any trader can benefit from learning and applying this theory in her or his daily work in the market place.

Chapter 9

THE STEIDLMAYER DISTRIBUTION

The building block of any market is its distribution—the basic unit of directional market movement. Although the term distribution had been associated with markets, the nature of market distributions has never been fully examined. In this chapter we discuss the Steidlmayer distribution, which is quite different from the more familiar normal distribution.

Purpose of Market

To understand the market, it is necessary to find its purpose. The real purpose of any market is to distribute a product efficiently, which is also its economic function. Any number of people trading among themselves without this purpose would not be serving society, and the market place would be doomed to failure. Trade facilitation is a measurement of activity that defines this purpose because it is volume. All activity takes place within a distribution. Just think of distribution as one would a company's market share. The purpose is to penetrate the market and gain an increasing share. The volume of activity would describe this. Also, try to think of the different support groups the company has to maintain and enhance its market share—warehouses, advertising, research, and the like. Analyzing any of these critical parts gives insight into the strength or weakness of the distribution. This represents the natural flow of information, and one wants to take the same approach to the markets. In other words, one wants to be inside the workings that support the market.

The Normal Distribution Versus the Steidlmayer Distribution

In the normal distributions, variables cluster around an average or mean value. When a normal distribution takes place in the market, prices center around the mean. Figure 9–1 is an example of a normal distribution. Notice that more time/price opportunities (TPOs) center around the mean price and there are fewer TPOs as one moves toward either price extreme. In the Steidlmayer distribution, prices again develop a range, but variables

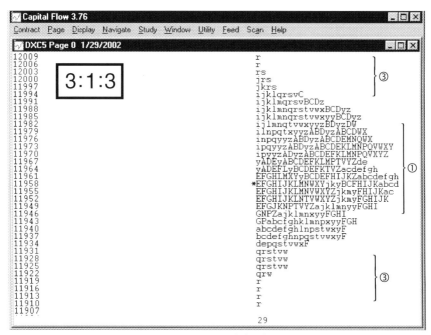

Figure 9–1   Normal distribution.

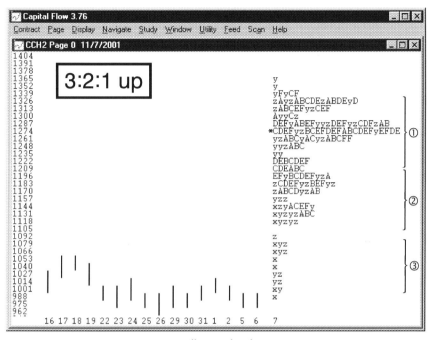

Figure 9–2 Steidlmayer distribution, 3:2:1 up.

Copyright © 1984 Chicago Board of Trade. All Rights Reserved. CBOT Market Profile, Market Profile, Liquidity Data Bank, and LDB are registered trademarks of the Chicago Board of Trade. All Rights Reserved. Provided by Steidlmayer Software Inc.

cluster toward one of the extremes within that price range. Note that in Figure 9–2 the mode (event with highest frequency of recurrence) is skewed toward the top of the vertical range, whereas in Figure 9–1 (normal distribution), the mode, which would also be the mean, is essentially in the middle of the vertical range. In a sense, a normal distribution is past tense, representing the filling out of a nearly completed distribution, whereas the Steidlmayer distribution represents the present tense development of an ongoing distribution. Later, it will usually be accumulated into a normal distribution pattern. Thus, a trader who is looking for the Steidlmayer distribution can have timely information from which to trade, rather than late information. She or he has a more efficient tool with which to take advantage of price when putting on a trade because she or he can take advantage of movements in the market on an informed basis.

The Steidlmayer distribution lends itself to opportunistic trading, for it presents a defined beginning or ending during which market prices fluctuate within the guidelines of the four steps of market activity discussed in Chapter 6. This phenomenon represents, I believe, the long-sought explanation of how professional traders can make money in what most academics believe is a totally efficient market. The Steidlmayer distribution is what all good traders perceive, although it has not been fully expressed or explained before. For a trader to have been consistently successful for a long period, he or she must be doing something right. The Steidlmayer distribution offers the explanation.

Illustrating the Steidlmayer Distribution

The visual imprint of the Steidlmayer distribution can be used interchangeably with the concept of the four steps of market activity discussed in Chapter 6. A Steidlmayer distribution would encompass the first three of the four steps of market activity. Those steps are a series of prices in one direction, trading to a price to stop the market, and finally trading around that stopping price. The distribution, the stopping, and the development around the stopping price are the essence of the Steidlmayer distribution.

From a visual standpoint, the Steidlmayer distribution resembles an uppercase "P" or a lowercase "b" (see Figs. 9–2 and 9–3, respectively). The size of the distribution can vary, as can its time frame. From a statistical perspective, these visual imprints are called either a 3:2:1 up (upper case "P") or a 3:2:1 down (lower case "b"). The numbers represent the first, second, and third standard deviations of a bell curve. In a normal distribution, a 3:1:3 bell curve (see Fig. 9–1), the first standard deviation appears in the middle of the range, with the second and third deviations falling above and below this median. This is the basis of the efficient market theory that a price away from value will always tend to move back to the center. This does occur in the market place from a very macro perspective; however, from the short-term perspective, this phenomenon occurs only in a nondynamic market

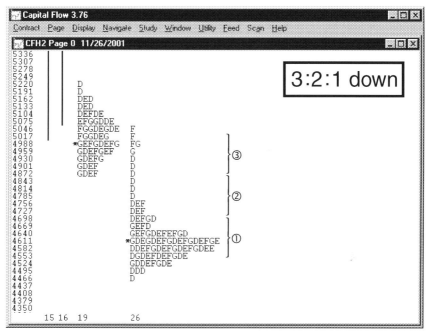

Figure 9–3 Steidlmayer distribution, 3:2:1 down.

where there is only development (horizontal price activity). On average, the historical price activity of a mature market is composed of a potpourri of 3:2:1s that make up a macro 3:1:3 structure. The markets do not make things easy. They do not present themselves in the neat little package of a 3:1:3, a money tree ripe for the picking. So the efficient market theory is not wrong; it is just a function of the time frame people are trading. The Steidlmayer distribution (3:2:1 up or down) is far more common in dynamic markets where movement is taking place. Traders can sense the existence of either type of distribution.

To help understand the four steps of market activity and assist in the visualization process of a 3:2:1 (Steidlmayer distribution) moving to efficiency (3:1:3), look at Figures 9–3 and 9–4. Figure 9–3 is a 3:2:1 down of the March coffee with the third, second, and first standard deviations denoted to the right of the profile. This profile looks something like a lowercase "b." What creates this type of visual is easily explained using the four steps of market activity. What creates the vertical range for the profile is step 1 (the distribution), a series of prices in one direction (down in this case). This strong push to the downside reaches a climax where there is little interest in continuing to sell lower prices; thus, the price probes lower and finally stop. The stopping of the distribution is step 2. Following the stopping phase, the market will probe both higher and lower, using the stopping price as a sort of anchor for development, or step 3. This development zone or step 3 in the four steps of market activity will constitute the first standard deviation of the Steidlmayer distribution. Once step 3 is established, the market will attempt to

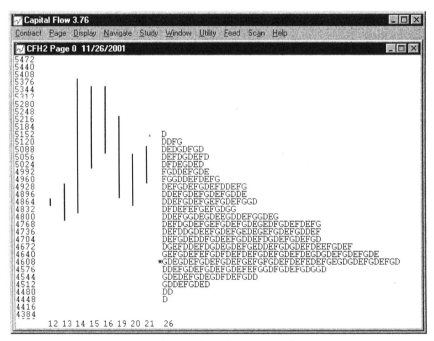

Figure 9–4   March coffee moves to efficiency.

move to step 4, which is the trade to efficiency (attempt to create a normal bell curve, 3:1:3), where the price activity attempts to move the first standard deviation back toward the middle of the vertical price range. How this occurred is shown in Figure 9–4, again March coffee fast-forwarded to include many more weeks of price activity. Once the market has stopped pushing in a direction (see Fig. 9–3), it attempted to retrace the selloff of 50 cents to 45 cents. The market managed to retrace that 5-cent selloff and then some; it eventually makes a new high versus what had been the high in Figure 9–3.

The Steidlmayer Distribution and Speed of Market Movement

When looking at the market from a daily perspective, only parts of the Steidlmayer distribution have the characteristic of being initiating or responsive in relation to the developing distribution—initiating in the second and third standard deviations, where the market moves quickly, and responsive in the first, where it moves more slowly. This relationship gives us the speed of market movement because the market will move quickly away from the third standard deviation but slowly away from the first. Another benefit of recognizing this distribution is that it contributes to the natural flow of information—information that is indisputable because the market is clearly either distributing or not distributing at any given time. The range of this distribution, along with the diversity of ownership and volume, gives us time; the greater the range, the diversity, and the volume, the more time we have. Just imagine the ability of a distribution to unwind, and the premise is clear. Suppose that 100 traders around the world buy soybeans, and the market moves up 8 cents a bushel. The market pauses in its distribution, and a few people decide to buy the pause, and a few others decide to take profits. Under these circumstances, the price will probably stay in the same general area. However, in the same situation, suppose that all of the 100 traders had the same purpose—say, to cover shorts—the same distribution could unwind fairly quickly. More rapid price change could then be anticipated.

Once the last short had bought to cover the position, the market could cascade lower if there was a lack of buying interest. OFI would give some objective information on how to trade this scenario.

Another example: Suppose 100 people buy the market, and the range is only 1 cent. If the market begins to move lower and all the participants are under water, one would expect many of them to sell at once; so the 1-cent range has not given them much opportunity for free exposure in the market. Although the participation was diversified, the small price range limited the opportunity to trade. The existence of the Steidlmayer distribution has been obscured by the fact that the larger time frame distribution often takes the appearance, after the fact, of a normal distribution. We call this push and pull of participants—coactive time frames (trading different durations). It is usually made up of several distributions that are profiled as one. In looking at this conglomerate, a trader is not getting pure, fast information but a blend; and a trader cannot successfully use blended information without making some adjustments. Working with pure information is the best way to build a database and adjust to changes in the markets.

Chapter 10

THE YOU

Because most of this book deals with the theory and development of Market Profile, one could assume that the few pages dedicated to the formula, Market Understanding × you = results, is of no particular importance. Such a conclusion would be presumptuous. They are equally important. Let us crunch the numbers and take a look. Assume 100 percent market understanding and the "you" component is operating only at 50 percent, your results would be 50 percent. If you flip the numbers around and market understanding is at 50 percent and the you component is running at 100 percent, again your results will be 50 percent. Both outcomes are the same. Thus, we should spend as much time developing the you component as you do developing the market understanding component.

A lot of people can look at a chart and generate a decent perspective of the market. They can even disseminate this information to others as the market unfolds exactly as they had envisioned. Upon complimenting the prognosticators on their accuracy in reading the market and inquiring into their profits from the trade, you find they made little or no money. Why? Their market understanding may be great but they do not have a handle on the you. They have personal issues they must overcome, until then they will be handcuffed.

Objectivity

A trader has one job—to be an objective observer of the market. This means she or he should observe the story being told by the market as it develops vertically and horizontally. When a good risk versus reward opportunity presents itself, a trader must take it. Then she or he continues to objectively monitor market developments.

One of the major shortcomings a trader can have is allowing one's opinions to take the place of objective market observation. The best traders are the ones who follow the lead of the market. The worst traders watch the market move against their position and rationalize the situation. Many a member has stubbornly stuck to a losing position, eventually blowing all his capital and losing his membership because the market could not possibly continue doing what it has been doing, and it does.

One sad example of this syndrome leaps to mind. Following the 1987 stock market crash and subsequent rally, one member of the Chicago Board of Trade would stand by the quote machine at the entrance to the trading floor and watch the Standard and Poor futures trading at the Chicago Mercantile Exchange. He was always short the market and regularly lost money. He would explain at great length to one and all why the market was going to resume its crash mode and make new lows. His fundamental arguments included deficit spending, high interest rates, and a plethora of other arguments. The fact the market continued to rally off the lows and trade through resistance level after resistance level never caused him to waiver. The inevitable eventually occurred and his membership was sold to cover his losses.

There are 101 ways to be a bad trader. But they all stem from an inability to maintain an analytical, objective viewpoint of the market. During the stress of the trading day, objectivity is often benched and replaced by any of these: anger, fear, jealousy, ambition, hesitation, uncertainty, overconfidence, laziness, depression, and countless other emotions. You as a trader want to be objective, but when you are playing a high-stakes game, your survival as a trader is always at stake to a greater or lesser degree. If you manage to be wrong big enough or long enough, you are out of the game. It is not hard to see why it is easy to get into situations in which decisions are not grounded in reason and logic.

Market Discipline

I converted the theoretical goal of being an objective observer into a nuts and bolts reality by developing a program that I now call market discipline. Market discipline has two components. The way I applied the first component is to study all my trades each day against the backdrop of what took place in the market—what I did, why I did it, why I was right or wrong. (Side note: to this day, one of the most successful futures traders in the industry keeps a daily journal of his trading. As a member of the Chicago Bulls, Michael Jordan practiced harder than any player on the team. Take their lead, strive to be the best you can be.) Market discipline included studying the relationship between background (long-term activity) and foreground (short-term activity), the internal contrast of the market within itself. An example would be that inefficiencies (vertical moves) are generally absorbed into an efficient background if they are not powerful enough to overcome the background. This became part of market discipline—studying the contrast between the short-term and the long-term to judge continuation. Doing this objectively by contrasting the relative vertical and horizontal dimensions is market discipline at work. Think of the tools discussed in Chapter 6 as tools in this effort to objectify market activity. One can make a daily chart comparing today's range, value area range, range extensions, buying and selling tails, and so on to the background. By doing so, one is allowing the market to objectively communicate. One is observing it—hopefully, being one with the market.

The second component involves the emotions I mentioned earlier in the chapter. Have you ever noticed how much easier it is to be objective about the markets when you are not involved? If one thinks about it, it is pretty clear why that would be the case. One is looking at the market without dealing with anger, fear, anxiety, excitement, and the like. Some of these emotions run on automatic and to say they complicate the decision-making process would be an understatement. They can overwhelm the decision-making process when the stakes get high enough.

There is only one way to overcome the ability of these emotions to possibly take over the show. When considering these emotions, do not limit the focus to fear and hesitation. Many a person has been hurt by overconfidence. Study your judgment under varying conditions—just like one would market activity. The best way to do this is to look at patterns in behavior. Do you make money only in the morning? What if you are not feeling well? Do you make money only in down markets? When you have a winner, does euphoria set in? Does the tension of holding a loser affect your judgment? Study yourself looking for understanding just like you would a market situation. Learn to accept what you see and work with it. Recognize your limitations. It is hard to turn a "slap" hitter into a 40 home run guy, just as it is hard to make a pull hitter go the opposite way. If your day starts out terrible, maybe you should consider quitting if you have a habit of making bad days into disasters. The same may apply when starting the day with a big winner; some people really press and give it all back.

One thing is clear. This is an exercise in self-discovery. No one is in a position to do a better job of studying yourself than you. After all, you are the only one who is with you 24 hours a day. It may not be easy, but it is necessary. You are looking for patterns. You are looking for tendencies that repeat themselves. When you are studying your daily trades looking for insights into why you are making or not making trades, look for emotional patterns as well.

You can learn what it takes to be a successful trader. You can attend every seminar in the book. But if you harbor some of these emotional flaws and they go undetected, you may be the smartest person on the block and never make a dime. It is all about understanding you.

Market discipline has many connotations. Practically speaking, it is the school of hard knocks. It means the market will punish those who try to fight it. It is a discipline that the market can and does impose on its participants. You learn by doing, by asking questions of yourself (e.g., why did I sell into a rally?; why are all my trades responsive?), by not repeating your mistakes, by taking responsibility for your actions, and by not complaining about what ifs, what went wrong, and so on. You are in a continual learning mode.

Market discipline is not a well-wrapped, pretty package. Learning from one's experience is not a neat and tidy process. It is not meant to be a 1- or 2-minute wrap-up at the end of the trading day. It is as much about you as it is the market. Learning means to gain knowledge or understanding of a subject. If you check a dictionary, you will see that the definitions of the word understanding include to comprehend and to be thoroughly familiar with the character and propensities of that which is being studied. No one in the world can improve you more as a trader than yourself. It is only through hard work and a willingness to come face to face with yourself as a trader that you will fully develop yourself and be able to achieve the results talked about in the equation for success:

$$\text{Market understanding} \times \text{You} = \text{Results}$$

Having a losing trade does not necessarily equate to an error on the part of the trader. The game is complex and the number of variables involved in trading preclude anything approaching perfection. Your job is to do whatever you can to improve your skills. It will improve your odds and your results. But if you never take the time to learn why you do what you do when you are trading, you have no chance of improving yourself—you are cutting your potential in half. Remember, the you is half the equation. If you apply yourself and learn to comprehend the propensities you have as a trader that are limiting your results, the trading experience can be a much more satisfying one. If you are half the equation, maybe you should get half the analysis.

Chapter 11

ANATOMY OF A TRADE

Up to this point, I have approached the process of trading as a foot-ball coach might prepare for Sunday's game—breaking down the offense and defense, and looking at line play and special teams; analyzing the skill positions, checking out key injuries, and tracking weather conditions; knowing what resources there are to work with and coming up with a game plan; being aggressive within the framework of the team's abilities, yet cognizant of the opponents' strengths to avoid the risk of running into a buzz saw.

You can implement a conservative or an aggressive game plan, statistically isolate situations in which certain plays should be run, even throw in some gimmick plays. Do you want to grind it out and play smash mouth football or go the finesse route and put on an aerial circus? Ultimately, the results should dictate your plan of attack. Are you winning or losing? Do you feel in control? To achieve the goal of winning, major and minor adjustments must be made throughout the game. At the end of the day, a horn sounds, the game is over, and there is a winner and a loser. Regardless of outcome, there is always next week, a time to redeem yourself or keep the momentum going.

Trading is no different. As a trader, you have certain skills and qualities that need to be honed through reading, educational seminars, and self-discovery. Is this not the same as an athlete going to practice to improve his or her skill set? What separates the winners from the losers is the ability to see the need to make an adjustment, the discipline to do so, and a willingness to follow through.

In this chapter, we help you formulate a game plan and show you ways to fine-tune your strategy. But remember, the respon-

145

sibility of making adjustments for the game falls squarely on your shoulders. Just as in athletics where coaches coach and players play, ultimately the players decide the outcome of the game. A trader needs to accept and form a personal covenant of responsibility for her or his trading decisions. Blaming others and deflecting responsibility is a guaranteed formula for failure.

The majority of this chapter revolves around recognizing a trade and attempting to execute that trade advantageously. First, however, I would like to leave you with one thought—the importance of ongoing education. Whether you are a trader, a doctor, or an electrician, the process of education can be done in the structured environment of a classroom, in a residency, or through an apprenticeship. Its purpose is to provide a foundation from which to build a future. The more unstable and dynamically changing the world is, the less secure the future. Therefore, more retooling or reeducating will need to be done. This book attempts to bridge the gap between the original Market Profile works and the new applications and concepts. Be aware that this is an ongoing process because the process of learning is never complete.

Game Plan

Now let us figure out a game plan. Applying what we have learned in a systematic fashion will help generate some trading ideas. Once again, the secret to successful trading is finding a quality opportunity and executing that opportunity under favorable conditions. Recall that three things can happen in the market: prices can trade higher, prices can trade lower, or prices can remain unchanged. Two out of three of these occurrences do not hurt you if you enter your trade (long or short) under favorable conditions. Thus, when you enter the market under favorable conditions you will have the chance to break even or be profitable two-thirds of the time. However, when you enter the market under unfavorable conditions (paying up to execute a trade when it is not warranted), your success ratio falls to one-third because the environment in which the market trades sideways will probably be a losing proposition as well. There are two parts to a trade, the idea and execution of the idea. A good trade always wins out, but what about the rest of the time?

Ideas can be fundamentally based, technically based, or based on intuition and gut feeling. If the explanation of fundamental trading is "dummied-down," we could say price is placed in the context of value and the trading decision is made from that platform. Fundamental traders generally trade one instrument or sector because an inordinate amount of material must be sifted through to gain perspective and stay current with market conditions.

Conversely, technical traders generate all their trades off charts and the interpretation of studies generated from those charts. Technical traders find a study or group of studies they are comfortable with and overlay those studies onto a database reflective of the time frame they want to trade.

The intuitive or gut trader is an altogether different animal. Quite often he or she cannot quantify what he or she does or why. In some fashion, he or she is subconsciously processing price, price relationships, news, and economic information to generate a trading idea. Unfortunately, this skill cannot be taught or modeled.

That being the case, let us go back to the first two entries on our list: fundamental and technical trading. Recall that fundamental trading is gaining an understanding of value and trading that perspective. Is that not exactly what the Market Profile is doing? A charting tool is used to organize price activity into a display (Market Profile) whose premise is the statistical bell curve or value. Therefore, Market Profile is a tool that straddles the technical and fundamental world of trading. By incorporating those two genres should that not make the trading tool better?

When trading ideas are being generated, the thought process should be systematic in nature. You do not want to trade on a whim or be reactive. In addition, for those trading more than one market, the approach should be relatively generic. By systematic, we mean going through a mental checklist (beginners may want to create an actual list) of things you look at to generate a trade. By generic, we mean applying the same approach or strategy to all markets you are trading. You may find nuances or tendencies for certain markets, but in general, stick to a blueprint over time. Work toward your strengths and keep things as simple as possible. "Play your game," do not succumb to outside pressures and do what everyone else is doing.

The game plan or blueprint I have built over time is:

• Work from background to foreground.
• Incorporate the visualization process to ascertain where you are within the four steps of market activity.
• Apply the internal time clock of the market to help supplement this information.
• Utilize day structure (range parameters, single prints, idiosyncrasies of markets) to optimize entry mechanism.
• Objectively mange positions (both winning and losing) with structure, not price.
• Control risk.
• Use stops.
• Vary size.

Now let us elaborate on this checklist. First of all, look at the background to determine the trend. As in all analysis, the world long-term or trend is related to the time frame you are trading. For a person scalping on the floor or screen, the trend may extend to the previous day's activity and nothing more. If you are doing something other than scalping, look farther out on the curve at hourly, daily, weekly, and monthly data to gain a longer-term perspective. However, as profile users, we are not proponents of chronological time as our organizational medium, but instead prefer to organize with market time.

That is where the next entry in our checklist comes into play: incorporating the visualization process with the four steps of market activity to determine where we are within the structure of the market. By looking at the internal time clock of the market (price/time relationship), we are able to accurately determine when the market is in a position to continue in the current direction, develop sideways, or reverse.

Continuing down the checklist, we find ourselves at a point in the exercise where we are essentially putting the price activity under the microscope to find a window of opportunity from which to trade. This is where we focus on day structure and our understanding of nuances within day structure in an attempt to optimize the entry mechanism.

With this checklist and the few short paragraphs we have used to elaborate on this process, we have summarized what has taken a lifetime to develop and improve. It will take some time to develop this thought process, but over time, you will find it becomes subconscious or automatic.

That moves us to the next topic on our checklist: trade management. Note that trade management is one entry in a list that numbers six or eight items. Proportionally, that represents something like 12 to 15 percent of the total material covered in the checklist. Surprisingly, that 12 to 15 percent is probably representative of the amount of time a trader spends managing a trade versus the process of generating and executing a trading idea. In other words, she or he spends seven-eights of the time coming up with the idea and one-eighth of the time managing the idea. In reality, a trader will be more successful if she or he reverses these numbers and spends more time managing the position (both good and bad) and less time anguishing over whether she or he should buy or sell and at what price. Earlier in this book, we called this metamorphosis of moving the responsibility of the trader from that of an observer to a manager the uplift process. Moving the entire checklist process to more of an objective automated format helps this transformation to occur.

The key word in the previous paragraph pertaining to trade management is objective—objective management of winning positions and losing positions in the context of the market structure and your trade plan. Just as in football, where the team goes into a game with a plan of attack based on film of opponents' previous games, the coach and players must then modify the game plan in the heat of the battle based on results. The same thing for the trader. She or he goes through the checklist creating a strategy based on structure and then must monitor and modify the game plan based on how the trade is unfolding. This does not mean picking a stop level based on some arbitrary risk factor and then calculating a profit objective based on some multiple of that dollar risk. No, assess the market, create a bias (long or short), optimize the entry mechanism (price), look at the structure to determine what type of price activity would negate your strategy, and then see whether the profit potential justifies the risk. It is almost like an accountant generating the bottom line first and then backing into the rest of the information to assess the business.

Remember, markets are dynamic; look at them as living, breathing organisms. Do not look at trades as an if/then statement, all or none, hit the profit objective or loss limit—be flexible, modify your game plan as you see fit.

Most importantly you want to control risk, be in a position to fight another battle. By controlling risk, we mean limit your losses. When markets of uncertainty are dealt with, there always is the chance of getting blindsided by some unexpected occurrence or news event. There is no way to anticipate this or trade for it. What we mean when we say control risk in trading is use some framework that features a disciplined approach to recognizing and taking losses.

Some people's answer to controlling risk is the use of stops. We are proponents of limiting losses; however, we do not necessarily believe a stop is the best means to that end. Anyone who has experienced trading has probably used a stop. It is the industry equivalent of a pacifier or baby blanket—something that creates a false sense of security. Do not get me wrong; the concept is great, however, the reality is jaded. Its purpose is to force discipline, the emotional quality that must be present for one to be successful in trading.

No one likes to admit he or she is wrong; it goes against human nature. Whether it is a wrong business decision, career decision, child-rearing decision, or trading decision, an individual given a choice will try to rationalize this decision. A trader may expand his or her timeframe, look to others for support of his or her idea, or rationalize away the adverse price movement with any of a hundred reasons in hopes of the market trading back to his or her price so he or she can become "whole" again.

Once the trader has set up a trading plan (entry, exit, and level he or she is wrong) and ultimately by taking the "choice" out of the hands of the participant and moving it to the market with a stop, the trader feels a false sense of security. How about the trader who was short new crop beans during the drought of 1988 with a 10-cent stop and the market was limit up 3 days in a row with no way out? Or the trader who was short Treasury bonds during the stock market crash of 1987 when the bonds were limit up for 3 or 4 days in a row? Or an experience I had being short the mini Standard and Poors 500 (S&P) with a 2-point stop when the Federal Reserve Board unexpectedly cut rates and my 2-point stop cost me 25 additional points ($1250/contract)? The list goes on and on.

Stops do not protect your capital as you might think. They are kind of like walking on ice wearing dress shoes; you can navigate around the ice most of the time, however, you will eventually hit that spot on the ice that puts you flat on your back. You do not know when or where it will happen, just that it will happen. Let market activity tell you when you are wrong, and put the responsibility of exiting squarely on your shoulders—you will do a better job.

The last entry on our list is probably the most overlooked and arguably the most important: adjusting the number of contracts you trade. In trading, you need to recognize an opportunity (by going through your checklist) and then to quantify that opportunity. By quantify, I mean rate the opportunity: is it a "run of the mill opportunity" offering typical returns on your trading efforts or is it one of those unique situations that could define your trading career? There is a saying "You pay the grocery bills with the day-to-day trading and put the money in the bank with the long-term trading." Similarly, most very successful traders will probably tell you they accumulated the majority of their wealth on a very small percentage of their trades. Looking at this idea from a value perspective, it would be a situation in which price is lagging value and you perceive a significant shift in value. In this situation, you should adjust your size to a much larger unit and really push the envelope.

Trade Setups

Now we go to finding trade setups. We advocate trading opportunities and not markets. Sinking a 10-foot putt with an uphill lie requires the same stroke for the golfer whether she or he is playing at Augusta National, Pebble Beach, Saint Andrews in Scotland, or the local park district course. Hitting a 90+ mph fastball delivered by Roger Clemens, Kerry Wood, or Randy Johnson requires bat speed and concentration. The trading game should be broken down and looked at in a similar vein. A portfolio of stocks and commodities should be "scanned" by the trader to locate setups that meet a predetermined criterion. At that point, the trades can be executed and managed. This common thread, or setup, for the trader is no different than the 10-foot putt for the golfer or the 90+ mph fastball for the baseball player. By breaking down trades in this manner, we are saying, "A trade is a trade is a trade, regardless of the market." If all our putts are 10-footers or we can sit back and look for the fastball on every pitch, we will perform better.

By tracking only a few markets, you will be limiting your trade opportunities. At some point, this will force you to trade outside your comfort zone—trying to make money when there is no clear setup. Early in your trading career, you want to build the "factory" no matter how mundane it may seem. Stick to a simple approach that can be expanded after you have built a base through observations and trading experiences. A golfer will score better keeping the ball in play and playing within her or his abilities. The baseball player will be more effective facing only fastballs; when the curveball, slider, and forkball are added to Randy Johnson's repertoire of pitches, the baseball becomes much more difficult to hit.

In going through trade examples, we are going to start at the lowest level and work to more complex applications. We are not holding ourselves out as sages or trading gurus using smoke and mirrors to generate trades. We are going to show you proven methods you can use to improve your trading. It will be up to the individual trader to decide what suits his or her needs and what his or her capacity is to understand and apply the concepts presented through the examples.

We are going to start off with our blinders on, push our nose up against the screen, and see only the bid and ask in the market. In trading, there is always a buyer for every seller; what causes price movement in any market is the holding imbalance of the participants. For this example, assume that I am the buyer, you are the seller, and both of us are trading a very short time horizon. The thing that differentiates us other than the side of the market we are trading is our individual conviction for the trade. Assume that I have a stronger conviction on this particular trade. I may let my trade go a number of ticks against me before I even consider liquidating the position. Conversely, you are short and have no opinion on the market. Your reason for putting on the trade was because you saw an edge and wanted to make a tick on the trade. Being short once the market goes bid, you will be falling all over yourself trying to scratch your position. In fact, if all the offers disappear, you will probably pay up to square up your position and lose a tick on the trade. All things being equal, my willingness to hold and your adversity to holding are what caused the market to move. (This example has been greatly simplified for the purpose of conveying the idea.) Thus, from even the shortest-term perspective, price movement is influenced by participant willingness to hold on to positions.

One relevant observation I have made pertaining to watching the book and order flow on my Trading Technologies (TT) front end is that when the book is stacked (aggregate bids vs. aggregate offers), the book is usually wrong. When I say stacked, I mean it has slightly less than twice as many total bids as total offers or slightly less than twice as many total offers as total bids. What is probably happening is a trader or traders on the wrong side of the market are putting in false bids or offers defending open position, which are cancelled once the market gets close to the trade price. This observation leads us into a very important lesson for a trader to learn early in his or her career—the importance of reading the market and not reacting. We have a saying, "Make price the messenger, not the message." Do not be reactive and jump at every price movement up and down; similarly do not make a casual observation and believe it is a lay-up trade. Incorporate price movement and order flow into a thought process in which you can trade. The thought process you develop is something you must be comfortable with or at the least be able to grow with over time.

Human Capacity

Trading the shortest time horizon is a very difficult way to trade in that you need to devote your full attention to the market with each and every tick. In addition, your level of performance, or what we call your "human capacity," needs to be running at the optimal level for an extended length of time. We all have done it for periods of time, and it is mentally and physically draining. A common experience many of us have had with human capacity running at optimal level would be taking an extremely challenging final examination in high school or college. I remember taking college finals in chemistry and calculus and how drained I was after taking the 3-hour examination that required my highest degree of concentration and effort. You get in a zone, blocking out all the noise and activity, focusing on the task at hand.

A friend on the floor of the Chicago Board of Trade (CBOT) has been doing just that for the past year. He stands in the pit with a Trading Technologies order routing system strapped to his chest, watching the orders come into the pit and the order flow traded on the screen. He trades 25 to 50 lots in the Treasury bonds, looking to get the edge whenever he can, and quickly lays off his position. He is always trying to read the order flow in both venues. He carries no positions overnight and consistently makes $20,000 to $100,000 a day. In my eyes, he is the Michael Jordan of scalping; however, just like Mike with age, injuries, and so on, your game starts to deteriorate and you lose a step. Once an athlete loses a step, he or she may transition to management, get involved in coaching or broadcasting, or move into another field.

Similarly, a trader who is running her or his factory at full capacity for an extended length of time will need to modify her or his program because it is physically impossible to maintain that level of concentration and effort. It will lead to burnout. Those who do not change their program become jaded, discouraged, and prone to failure.

Volume Studies

A derivative of this very short term program can be run utilizing one of the volume studies mentioned earlier in this book. Recall that on floor information (OFI) gives Capflow32 users the skew of filled buy orders versus filled sell orders generated from off the floor. This gives us a perspective as to what the big barn boss is doing. We use the term big barn boss as if it were an individual, but in reality it is the group (buyers or sellers) whose coattails you want to latch onto. Floor traders try to garner the same information when surveying the pit, and screen-based traders seek the same information when looking at the book (accumulated bids and offers in an array of prices above and below the market). A floor trader's is a subjective read of the market real time; OFI is an objective read of the market after it is closed. Which is better? The floor trader's if the read is accurate because it is real time. However, we are unable to work from the base of having timely participant biases, so we will work with what we have. As we stated earlier, OFI gives a bias for the first hour or hour and a half of trade following the day it is generated. Thus, we have a tool for the short-term trader to use that eliminates one side of the market for part of the session. Incorporate that with some of the early entry tools that were part of the original Market Profile approach and you have a strategy to work with.

The original Market Profile works taught us there were two types of early entry price activity that could be objectively read and traded, both of which were generated off the opening price of the session and the next few minutes of trade. Early entry buying and early entry selling are the activity we are referring to. In a chronological database, there is meaning and importance to opens as well as to closes. We define early entry buying as opening and driving higher from the opening price and early entry selling as opening and driving lower from the opening price. This early entry activity could be combined with OFI to create a system for trading the openings. For instance, let us assume we have OFI buying of 1.25 and our experiences tell us that any number greater than 1.2 is reliable. Seeing early entry buying on the tail of this OFI number would be the trigger to initiate a long position.

Figures 11–1 and 11–2 are precisely the setup to look for to have early entry activity confirmed by strongly biased OFI numbers. Figure 11–1 is a screen capture of the September 5-year note with the OFI numbers affixed to their respective profile. In the fixed income markets, our studies show anything greater than 1.25 or less than 0.75 is statistically significant and therefore

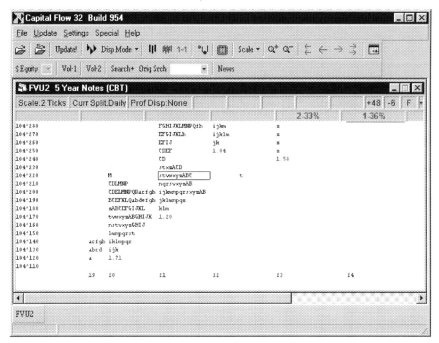

Figure 11–1   September five-year note with the OFI numbers affixed to the respective profile.

Copyright © 1984 Chicago Board of Trade. All Rights Reserved. CBOT Market Profile, Market Profile, Liquidity Data Bank, and LDB are registered trademarks of the Chicago Board of Trade. All Rights Reserved. Provided by Steidlmayer Software Inc.

should be incorporated into one's thought process. Note the reading of 1.71 affixed to the bottom of the profile dated the 20th. This number tells us that the filled order flow coming from off the floor was strongly skewed toward large buy side tickets. This information is made available from the exchange after the close so it is useful for trading the night session or the next day's morning session. Seeing strongly skewed OFI numbers like this should serve as an alert to watch the next morning's opening activity.

Figure 11–2 is a daily profile display of the referenced OFI display. The reason the profiles do not appear to be filled out is because the futures contract was not front month at the time. With an OFI reading of 1.71 on May 20, we would be looking to play the market from the long side early on the morning of May 21. Looking at the profile display on May 21, you can see the early entry activity characterized by opening and pushing in a direction down or up in this case. Looking at the profile dated May 21 in Figure 11–2, you see a small triangle to the left of the "y" period at the price of 104.29. This represents the opening price for the session. The triangle to the right of the profile represents the closing price of that day's activity. Thus, on May 21, you can see the market opened at 104.29 and never traded lower than that price throughout the day. On that day, the market closed at 105.04. Incorporating OFI with the early entry buying activity would have been the signal to play the market from the long side on May 21.

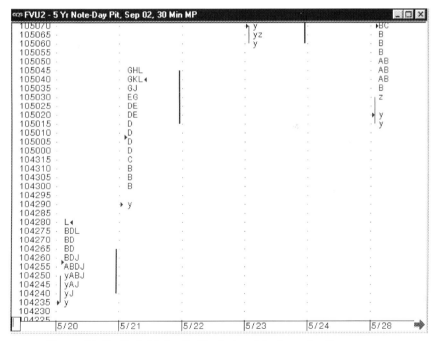

Figure 11–2 Daily Market Profile display of the September five-year note.

This is not to say that early entry or OFI should be used only for scalping purposes. A friend who was the biggest trader on the London International Financial Futures Exchange (LIFFE) floor used this trade setup for years with great success. A pattern he noticed was that on the first day of the week the German bund would have an open and drive–type setup. He would watch the open to determine direction and initiate a position with a stop a few ticks through the opening price. If the trade was working for him, he would hold it to the open of the U.S. market and possibly to the close of the European markets. Prior to this year (2002), this strategy worked over 70 percent of the time for him.

Utilizing a Chronological Data Base

Maintaining our focus on chronological databases, we move up a rung to find a slightly more advanced strategy, yet one still easy to read and manage. In so doing, we want to keep in mind that our purpose is to build a business, chip away, and develop some consistency, not strike it rich going for the long ball. We want to be able to read the market, see an opportunity, act on it and then reload. At times we will be right, other times wrong, but most importantly we will be in the game tomorrow. We are trying to create a blueprint or business plan for our trading business. To do this, we must have a core strategy and we need to monitor trends in the industry to determine whether the core strategy needs to be modified. The strategy we present at this time involves utilizing a chronological database with the expectation that the condition of the market is random. In other words, we are looking for some degree of horizontal development to persist.

In a chronological database, trending activity occurs approximately 10 to 20 percent of the time and development or sideways trade accounts for the other 80 to 90 percent of price activity. Thus, from an involvement perspective, we should skew our participation, or more accurately our participation expectation, to 80 percent of the time looking for random activity and 20 percent of the time looking for nonrandom activity. If the market is random four-fifths of the time, an intelligent strategy might be to trade for the norm and anything that exceeds the norm may fall into the trending-type activity, which will be a loser for us.

A friend trading on the floor of the CBOT in the early 1980s traded this strategy in a convoluted sort of way. An up and coming star at the time by the name of Richard Dennis was known for his aggressive breakout trading style. My friend would follow Mr. Dennis around the floor and try to gauge when he was finished initiating his position and then fade him. The idea being that markets broke out only 10 to 20 percent of the time (when fading breakouts did not work), so if risk controls were in place for the 10 to 20 percent of the time when the market trended, there was a good chance to net money on the other trades (when fading breakouts worked). What made this strategy even more effective was that Richard Dennis became such a well-capitalized local and fund manager that locals stepped back when he came into the market. Therefore, his buy orders saw fewer offers and his offers saw fewer bids, creating even more price movement and a better price for anyone fading his order flow.

Trading Parallel Activity

Unfortunately, we do not have a strategy as easy to apply as this, but we present something that looks to capture markets in the development phase, the strategy being to trade parallel activity. When trading parallel activity, we look for some type of standard or normal range of prices to recur for the time frame we are monitoring. Assuming the market is in development or randomness, this pattern has a high probability of occurring.

How does it work? Essentially, you are looking for today's price range to be approximately the same number of ticks as the previous day's price range. In other words, you are calculating some type of average daily range. Once this measurement objective has been met, participants can look for the high and low to be in for the day and trade accordingly. This approach can be expanded beyond the day to look at weekly parameters as well.

Realizing that you are looking for one thing, and one thing only, there should be no need to second-guess yourself or find other reference points to support your idea and stay with the position. Your strategy did not work out, so get out and look for other opportunities.

Figure 11–3 is a daily Market Profile display of American Express. The first observation that comes to mind is the degree of congestion or overlapping prices that occur over the 6 days of profiles. When seeing this type of price activity always look for parallel activity. Parallel activity indicates some degree of stopping and development as described in the four steps of market activity. From a daily perspective, a precursor to this type of activity might be a preponderance of neutral activity (neutral days) or, from a structural standpoint, the market reaching a maturity level greater than 19 (wide time/price opportunity [TPO] point) based on the internal time clock of the market. At this point, we can objectively say the near-term structure has begun to lose

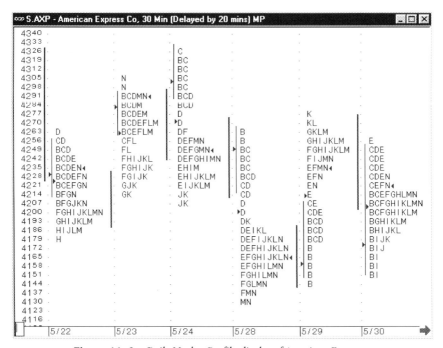

Figure 11–3   Daily Market Profile display of American Express.

momentum and we should trade some type of mean reversion. The tool of choice to trade a mean reverting program is trading parallel activity because it most accurately gauges potential price ranges. Anticipating some form of price control allows you to implement what we call a hit and run trading style, in that one piece of information is being extracted from the market and traded. This very aggressive style must be given a short leash when it comes to trade management. Let us look to Figure 11–3 to help understand this idea. By looking for parallel activity, we are saying we expect the current day's activity or price range to mirror the range of the previous day. Looking at the profile on May 22, we can see the approximate price range was 41.80 to 42.60, or 80 cents. Thus, if we can make a case for the next day's activity to be some sort of mean reverting activity, we can look for something close to an 80-cent range for May 23. This approach does not give us any trade opportunities out of the box; however, other indicators may signal a trade price, and then parallel activity could be used as the objective or exit for the trade. In the case of May 23 let us assume we have no reason to sell the market early in the day. Instead, halfway through the day, we see the market has met one of our range parameters off day structure, which is a normal variation day objective of doubling the first hour's range. The first hour's range or initial balance (B and C periods) was six ticks (using the chart's default price scale). Adding that same six-tick range to the bottom of the first hour's range would project the market down to 42.14, the low of the day. Based on that information, a long position could be generated with a parallel day objective off the previous day's 80-cent range. Thus, if we are able to buy near the low of the day on May 23 at the price of 42.14 and we tack that 80-cent expected range onto the day's low to give us an upside objective of 42.94. On May 23, the buying did creep into the market during the second half of the day, allowing for a trade all the way up to 43.05, exceeding our parallel day objective by about 10 cents. Note that the day's activity eventually unfolds into a neutral day (first hour's range extended to the upside as well as the downside) after meeting a normal variation day objective. This observation is very meaningful in that it tells us something beyond the day structure is controlling price activity. This is the underlying reason our entire methodology has evolved from day structure and a chronological database to a market activity database. Using the same point and shoot trading style (generating a trade off a single piece of information or trading tool), this same parallel day strategy on May 24 versus May 23 would have you looking for a similar 80-cent range. When the market breaks 80 cents from the day's highs of 43.26 down to 42.46, a buy signal would have been triggered. The market stopped near that price momentarily (42.42) during the D period and then liquidated another 35 cents.

Continuing with Figure 11–3 and applying the strategy of trading parallel activity, the strategy works when using the $1.20 range on May 24 as our proxy for the days range on May 28. On May 28, you would be buying American Express at the parallel day objective of 41.40. Going into the close, the market is trading at 41.65; at that point we have two choices: hold the position overnight or take a 25-cent profit. Realizing that the market is in development, the decision should be simple: hold.

When the market is in the development mode, the auction process will be to trade to a price too high to shut off the buying and then trade to a price too low to shut off the selling. Once the market has set the high and low boundaries, it will trade within that range until it reaches full maturity and then it can move vertically again. By holding the long position generated on May 28 at the price of 41.40 and using the $1.20 parallel day measurement parameter, we would be tacking that $1.20 to the low of the day's range of 41.44, which would give us a measuring objective of 42.64 on May 29. Getting out of the long and reversing to go short at 42.64 would be a good strategy because the market continues to show all the hallmarks of development.

In this example, we focused on trading day structure with the concept of parallel activity. Applying or looking for parallel activity in any chronological database has merit. It is a good practice to slow down the database and apply this same approach to weekly, monthly, or longer time frame activity. When applying this approach to weekly activity, we need to be a bit less exact in our measurements because the extended duration brings in additional stability that may dampen the magnitude of the third standard deviation and not allow for the exact prices to be met.

Trading Day Structure

The next strategy to be covered was used in the early days of Market Profile as a stand-alone strategy. Over time, this strategy has evolved to something that in most cases is used in conjunction with other tools. The strategy I am referring to is trading day structure. In the early to mid 1980s, when the Market Profile was first introduced, traders would do nothing more than go with any extension beyond the first hour's range, and there was a very good chance one of the supplemental range parameters of normal, normal variation, or trend day would ensue. The primary reason this strategy worked in the 1980s was because most of the participants were day traders, and therefore, it became almost a self-fulfilling prophecy. However, as time passed and other longer-term participants came into the picture, this go with strategy of trading day structure no longer worked. It became more difficult for day traders to push the market out of line and reach supplemental range parameters because longer-term players were always there to keep the market in line. Currently, I use day structure to manage existing positions; however, I seldom initiate positions with day structure (with the exception of trend days and neutral days).

Figure 11–4 is a Market Profile display of a stock traded on the London Stock Exchange (LSE) by the name of Electrocomponents PLC. The one-dimensionality (trending-type activity) or environment in which day time frame participants overwhelm the market is evident from a day perspective and thus very tradable from an objective standpoint. To refresh your memory, a nonrotational market and a close within 10 percent of the vertical extreme (high or low) characterize a trend day. By nonrotation, we mean unchanged to higher highs and higher lows for a trend day up and unchanged to lower lows and lower highs for a trend day down. This pattern may be broken once or at most twice within the day and still maintain some type of trend day. The strategy here is very simple: make the trade with the trend using 2 half-hour countertrend rotations as the signal that the market is moving from directional to stopping. Looking at Figure 11–4, which is a trend day down in Electrocomponents PLC, you should be looking to sell with the trend. If, within the day,

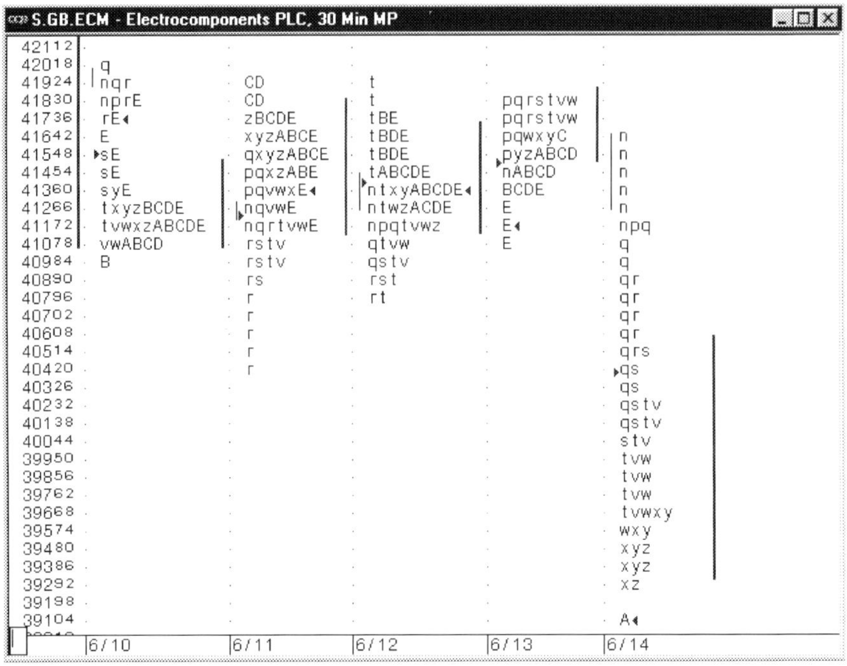

Figure 11–4   Electrocomponents PLC.

you see more than 2 half-hour up rotations, assume the market has lost the strong selling momentum, and thus get out of your short position. If you are involved with this type of trade, always exit by the close of a trend day because there is some 90 percent chance the market will trade sideways or reverse that day's price activity the next day. Figure 11–5 is a daily Market Profile display of the September Treasury bonds. Note that 3 of the 4 days displayed are trend days (the profile on May 9 is a neutral day). On May 8, we see a trend day down with the standard characteristics (nonrotational, close near the extreme). Based on our understanding of trend-type profiles, we would be looking for May 9 to be a sideways to up day. The neutral day pattern of that day would fall within that category. On May 10, we see a trend day up with one countertrend half-hour rotation and a close on the high of the day. Expecting stopping or reversing activity the following day would have us selling the close on May 10 or executing one of my favorite strategies of selling slightly out of the money calls. Premiums would be pumped up, and barring a gap higher open, selling volatility would be money in the bank.

The type of day structure I trade most aggressively because it gives very specific entry, exit, and stop levels is the neutral day. As opposed to the trend day, which features one-dimensionality and day time frame participants overwhelming the market, the neutral day features the opposite extreme—longer time frame participants are active and the market is random or developing. Trading for neutral structure can be anticipatory or totally objective, depending on how aggressive you wish to be. For instance, all markets have certain idiosyncrasies that can be

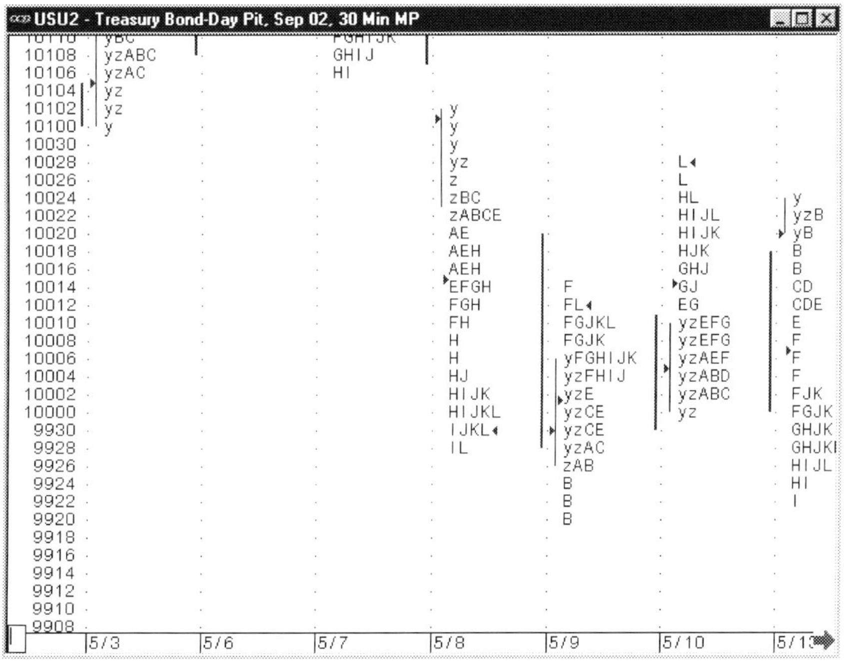

Figure 11–5 September Treasury bonds.

learned over time through observation. I have noticed that if a market is going to unfold into a neutral day, the expansion above or below the day's first hour of activity typically will not exceed "x" number of ticks. In the Treasury bond, I have noticed that 4 ticks is the outer boundary of expansion that one can lean against with some degree of reliability. If I come into the day and my read of the market is development, I may look to fade the first four-tick expansion above or below the first hour's range. On the first profile, dated April 10 in Figure 11–6, you can see that the C period took out the low of the initial balance (99.03) by exactly four ticks. The day trading participants have extended the market directionally; now it is time for the longer-term participants to step in, capping off the market as price becomes stuck in development. Assuming the longer-term participant

```
USU2 - Treasury Bond-Day Pit, Sep 02, 30 Min MP
9925 ·        H        DHI              yKL           · F
9924 ·        GHI      DH               yKL           · FG
9923 ·        EGHI     D                zK            · FG
9922 ·        EFGHI    D                zK            · FG
9921 · G      DEGHI    D                zK            · FG
9920 · G      DEGHIK   D                zK            · FG
9919 · G      DEIK     C                zK            · FG
9918 · G      CDIK     BC               zAK           · FG
9917 · G      CDIJKL◄  yB               zAK           · FG
9916 · G      CDJL     yAB              zAHJ          · FG
9915 · FG     CDJ      yAB              AGIJ          · FG
9914 · yFI    C        yzAB             AIJ           · FG
9913 · yFJ    zAC      yzAB             BCIJ     zB   · FG
9912 · yFJ    zAC      yzAB             BCIJ     zB   · FG
9911 · yFJ    yzABC    yzA              BCEIJ    zABC · FGJ
9910 · yFJ    yzAB     yz               BDEJ     zABC   FGJ
9909 · yDFJ   yzAB     yz               DE       zABCD  FGJ
9908 · yDEJKL yzAB     z                DE       zABC · FGJ
9907 · yADEJKL y       z                D        zBC  · FGJ
9906 · yABDKL◄ y       z                         zBCE · FGJ
9905 · yzABCDK y                                 zBCE · FGI◄
9904 · yzABCDK y                                 zBCE   CFGH
9903 · zAC    y                                  BCEF   BDFG
9902 · AC     y                                  BCEFG  BDFG
9901 · C      y                                  BEFH   BDFG
9900 · C                                         EFHK   BDEH
9831 · C                                         EHIKL  ABDE
9830 ·                                           HIJKL◄ ABD
9829 ·                                           HJ     A
9828 ·                                           HJ     z
9827 ·                                           H    · z
9826 ·                                           H    · z
9825 ·                                           H    · z
       4/10    4/11    4/12   4/15    4/16    4/17    4/1
```

Figure 11–6   September Treasury bonds.

can overwhelm the shorter-term, the expansion beyond the first hour's range will fail and "suck" back into the day's development. In fact, what typically happens is that the price probe that fails encourages day time frame participants to enter when an excess is in place and they feel the market may be poised for a vertical move in the other direction. Lo and behold, the market does probe the other end of the first hour's range, expands the range by approximately the same number of ticks as the first expansion, only to find the longer-term participant again limiting the price probe. This is what I call a symmetrical neutral day, equidistant price probes on either side of the first hour's range, with an eventual close near the middle of the day's range as both short-term buyers and sellers have used all their bullets and opt for returning to play the game tomorrow.

The leftmost profile in Figure 11–6 displays two of the three characteristics I mentioned. There was a four-tick extension beyond the first hour's low, which should be bought at 98.31/99.00 with an initial objective of a four-tick expansion above the first hour's high of 99.14. Looking to exit the long at that symmetrical neutral day objective of 99.18 did see further expansion to the upside by some three ticks and then a trade back down and close near the middle of the day's range.

As you can see, any order in which you enter in this strategy (anticipating first failure due to idiosyncrasies of underlying), objectively trading second expansion based on degree of first, and looking for a trade back to the middle of the day's range at a minimum are all clearly defined levels that can be defended quite objectively with the use of a stop.

As with parallel days, neutral days indicate some type of balance in the market. Looking for balance can be expanded beyond daily to weekly activity at a minimum. When looking for neutral activity from a weekly perspective, I use the Monday/Tuesday range as the initial balance and the rest of the week to measure expansions beyond that range. To gain an understanding of how to look at structure from a weekly perspective, look at Figure 11–7, which displays 1 week's activity in the first five profiles for the stock AOL. The first two profiles, which are Monday and Tuesday of the week, have a range of 17.10 up to 18.12. The subsequent price activity pushes higher on Wednesday and Thursday (third and

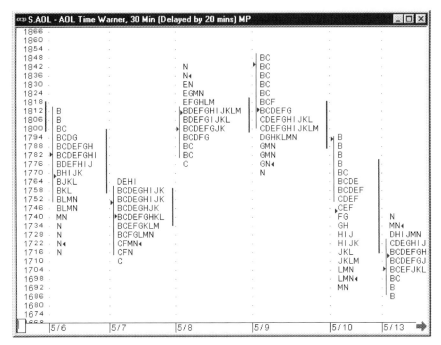

Figure 11–7   AOL Time Warner.

fourth profiles of the display) up to the price of 18.48. The market then fails the second half of the day on Thursday (5/9) and continues lower on Friday (5/10), taking out the Monday/Tuesday lows by some 20 cents. This was not a perfectly symmetrical neutral week because the high of the weekly initial balance was taken out by about 40 cents and the lows by only 20 cents. However, seeing the market fail back through the highs of the week, shorts would have been given some type of measuring objective to shoot for.

Auction Points and Single Prints

The next three groups of activity we focus on are a function of other time frame participants' involvement in the auction process. The output or price levels generated are very objective and easy to interpret. The three groups are (1) auction points from range extensions, (2) auction points from failed range extensions, and (3) single prints. To refresh your memory, an auction point is a function of longer-term participants entering the market and expanding the range beyond the initial balance (first hour) range. It is called an auction point because that is the level at which participants must step up to the plate. Subsequent price activity and the daily close have meaning within the confines of a chronological database. A confirmed auction point is when the closing price is outside the initial balance range (prices closing above the auction point to the upside or prices closing below the auction point to the downside). This type of price activity and close confirms that the longer-term participants who created this phenomenon of trading outside the first hour's range (thus creating an auction point) are seeing their perspective validated.

The flip side of this trade would be a failed range extension. Everything remains the same as far as setting up the initial balance and having the longer-term participants entering the market with a bias and moving prices in that direction, creating an auction point. The auction point to the upside is the specific price one tick above the first hour's high, and the auction point to the downside is the specific price one tick below the first hour's low. The word failed in failed range extension comes into play when the close does not confirm the auction point. For instance, a close below the auction point to the upside or a close above the auction point to the downside is considered a failed range extension. The buying above or selling below did not hold.

What are the implications of either type range extension? The specific auction point price should be seen as a level of support or resistance for later trade. Logic tells us that if participants moved prices outside the first hour's range and they were rewarded, that level will be noted and they will trade that price again if the opportunity arises. Conversely, if longer-term participants move prices outside the first hour's range and prices fail, the longer-term participant initiating this momentum trade has been burned and next time he or she sees these prices, he or she will more than likely play fade instead of go with.

Let us look at a few examples to illustrate this point. Figure 11–8 is a daily Market Profile display of the October live cattle. Let us focus on the profiles for June 3 and 5 (dates along bottom of screen) to show how to trade failed range extensions. The thin vertical line to the left of the daily profile represents the initial balance range (first hour's trade). On June 3, you can see that participants pushed prices above the first hour's high, creating an auction point to the upside at the price of 6550 during "E" period. The closing price for that day, which is denoted by the small triangle to the right of the day's profile, is 6520. Closing below the auction point of 6550 means we have a failed range extension at the price of 6550 and that price should be referenced as a sell level when the opportunity arises. The following day (6/4) the market opened near this price and sold off 2 cents over the next 2 trading days.

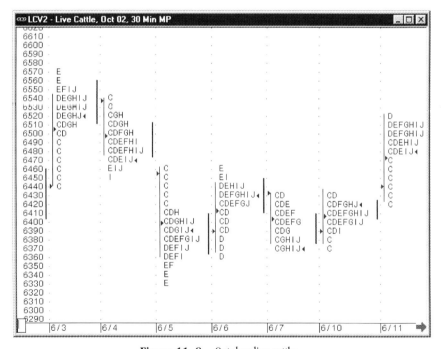

Figure 11–8   October live cattle.

Looking at Figure 11–8 again, we have another failed range extension day on June 5. The auction point to the downside was 6360 and the market closed at 6390. Initiating sellers got burned with the momentum trade that day, so at the next opportunity to trade that price, they will flip their trading card over and attempt to buy 6360. On the following day (6/6), 6360 was the low of the day, and within 4 days, the market was 1.5 cents higher. One thing I have noticed about failed range extensions is their propensity to occur near tops and bottoms of market development. If you think about it, that makes total sense because the longer-term participant is trying to move prices away from the day structure and a longer-term structure, and if he or she fails, you have both a daily and a longer-term failure. I recommend applying this strategy to weekly analysis with Monday/Tuesday representing the initial balance and watching the Friday close to give a perspective as to confirmation or failure.

Now let us go over an example of a held range extension to help solidify the concept. Figure 11–9 is a daily Market Profile display of Philip Morris generated from Capital Flow 3.76. Focus on the leftmost profile with the horizontal line through the profile at the price of 53.85. The line and corresponding price indicate the auction point to the upside (took out the high of the initial balance) for June 16. The closing price is not denoted on this display; however, "N" is the last period of the day and the N period's range is 54.30 to 54.60—thus, the market closed above the auction point to the upside at 53.85. The following day, the market opened unchanged and sold off to the auction point up of 53.85, traded through that price by a few cents, then bounced. Figure 11–10 is the same chart in daily bar chart form. Use the reference of the horizontal line that bisects the vertical bars on June 16 and 17 as your auction point of 53.85. From that point, the market rallies $4.00 (almost 8%) over the next 12 trading days. In the examples you have seen so far, the auction points have been tested rather quickly; however, that is not always the case. At times, it may be weeks or longer before these points are tested; continue to trade these levels until they are violated and fail.

Now to trading one of the most objective outputs of the market, single prints. Single prints within a profile are a form of mi-

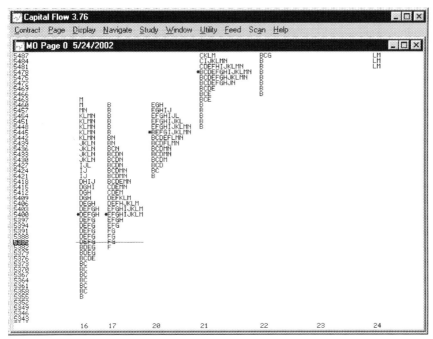

Figure 11–9   Philip Morris with auction points denoted by horizontal line.

nus development. By minus development we mean lacking development. Under normal market conditions, price activity falls into some type of normalized bell curve. The auction process of trading too high to shut off the buying and too low to shut off the selling serves the function of taking volatility out of the market. On average, once the volatility is removed, something happens (i.e., economic, fundamental, or technical event) that brings the volatility back. At times, the market deviates from this vertical, backing and filling, vertical phenomenon and we only see the vertical (backing and filling is skipped); at that point minus development is in place. Unopposed buying or selling (single prints) is what we call minus development. As you collapse more data together to create a longer time frame, you are essentially removing the volatility or minus development. To illustrate this point, we start by looking at a daily Market Profile display of the Dow futures contract traded on the CBOT. In Figure 11–11, the single prints on the profile of June 28 have been referenced by the pair of horizontal lines originating from that day's profile. On the previous 2 days (6/23 and 24), the market was relatively contained, with the daily lows occurring at about the same price. In other words, the price probes lower were met by buying that caused the market to rotate up and maintain some degree of price control. On June 28, the market opened within the price control range of the previous 2 days, probed lower, and found no buying. The unopposed selling allowed for single prints to be created in the profile as the market price trended lower, causing a shift in value of the underlying instrument. The remainder of the day (some of which is not displayed) developed in

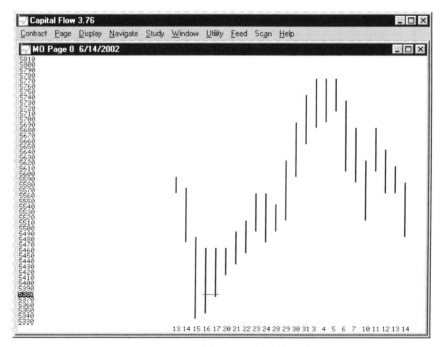

Figure 11–10 Philip Morris daily bar chart.

Provided by Steidlmayer Software Inc.

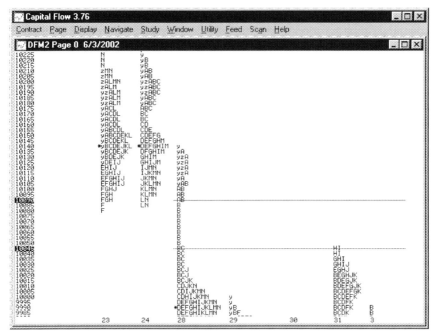

Figure 11–11   Dow futures on Chicago Board of Trade.

the lower quarter of the day's range. Owing to scaling issues, the next 2 days of price activity are not displayed. The following day (6/31) mounted a rally and attempted to trade up into the single prints where aggressive selling entered the market and quickly overwhelmed the buying. Owing to scaling, it is not evident that the single prints were violated by a few ticks then prices fell away. To help you appreciate the magnitude of the move that followed, we have displayed the Market Profile chart in a daily bar format. In Figure 11–12, the single prints have been referenced by a pair of horizontal lines originating from that day's price area. During the following three sessions, the market was able to probe the single print area on only one occasion (the third day) and quickly fell away. The muted probe into this area indicates underlying weakness in the Dow futures contract. Con-

ceptually, single prints should be looked at as market techni-
cians view a gap in price activity, something that has been created and needs to be tested. The speed at which the area is tested
and the magnitude of the retest give us some insight to the hand
the participants are holding. The stronger or more confident
hand will allow for a shallower retracement into the single
prints; a weaker or waning opinion will allow for a deeper retracement or filling of the single prints. In this case (Fig. 11–12),
the subsequent price activity makes a muted attempt (only
trades into single prints by a few ticks) at retracing into the single prints, telling us there is a great deal of underlying weakness
in the market. This being the case, you might think the potential sell off would be quick and large. Lo and behold, the sell off

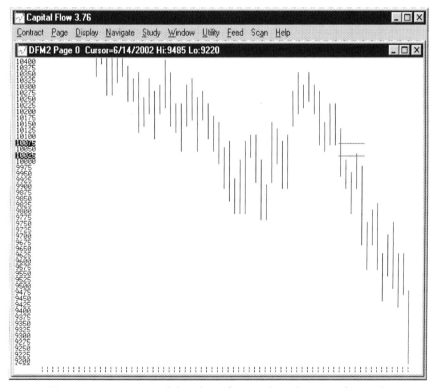

Figure 11–12   Dow Daily bar chart of Dow with single prints referenced.
Provided by Steidlmayer Software Inc.

originating from the single prints of 10,050 bottomed out at around 9200, equating to $8,500 profit on trading a one lot.

Background Versus Foreground

Needless to say, every setup is not as clear or profitable as this one but all are worth considering. By understanding the market dynamics of equilibrium, disequilibrium, you are able to look at each individual scenario and ascertain the potential of each. When attempting to determine whether a market is in equilibrium, you look at both foreground and background information to come to some consensus. The first generalization you can make is that the background dominates the foreground. Only when the background is in equilibrium can the foreground dominate. When both background and foreground are in equilibrium or both are featuring different biases, you have no opportunity. However, when the background and foreground line up, you have both time frames on your side, expecting a bigger vertical move. A logical question that might arise from this discussion is what is the background and the foreground. The answer to this question lies with the user. The macro trader or specialist on the floor would have different definitions of background and foreground. In summary, trading single prints offers a great opportunity because it puts you on the outer edge of recognizing minus development. The shallower the retracement into single prints, the greater the probability of a larger vertical move away from this area. Risk should be managed to the other side of the single prints because taking away all the single prints would signal a market in equilibrium or price control, which is not what we are trading for.

Creating a High Level of Trading

What we have done to this point, is bring you up to speed in finding trade setups and managing those trades. This process has featured singularity of focus, or singular inputs to generate a trade. What needs to be done to move you to a higher level of trading is move your thought process up a level or two. No longer do you want to incorporate point and shoot trading, but instead want to use the basic programming language of if/then to create simple trading programs. This if/then approach can be seen as a filter to uplift your program to a higher level of output. This systematic approach should be applied in a dynamic fashion; as your trading knowledge and experience grows, you should be incorporating this newfound information into your program. In addition, markets are always changing; therefore, what works today may not work tomorrow.

Integrating information to create some type of system can be as broad-reaching as the user desires. Your program may be as simple as using the background information generated from a composite profile, finding minus development (single prints) within the structure, and narrowing your focus to the day structure to locate an attractive price for order entry. Figure 11–13 illustrates this type of setup. Note how we have combined many

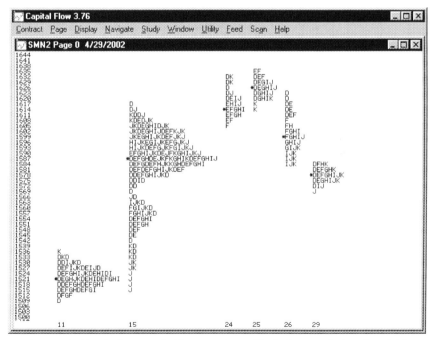

Figure 11–13 Soybean meal with composite profiles built on April 11 and April 15. Copyright © 1984 Chicago Board of Trade. All Rights Reserved. CBOT Market Profile, Market Profile, Liquidity Data Bank, and LDB are registered trademarks of the Chicago Board of Trade. All Rights Reserved. Provided by Steidlmayer Software Inc.

days' worth of price activity to create larger profiles (composite profile). The left-most profile encompasses 2 or 3 days' worth of price activity and would be categorized as price control or balanced. The composite profile with the single prints embedded in the structure is showing a form of minus development. Visually the composite is a 3:2:1 to the upside, a precursor to further upside probes. As the market breaks down toward the single prints, your radar should be up looking for some type of buy signal within the day structure. In Figure 11–13, the right-most profile features day structure conducive to buying. The reason I say this is because the previous day's profile is a trend day down, which is not good for follow through. Taking it one step further, let us look at Figure 11–14 in a one-tick scale. Note the right-most profile dated April 29, with the first hour's range (D and E peri-

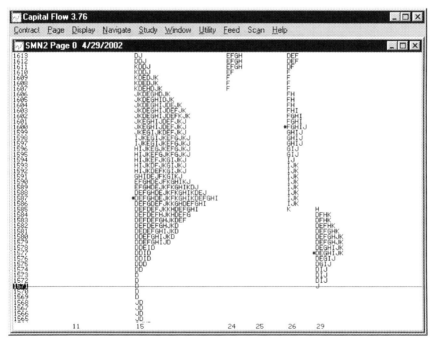

Figure 11–14   Market Profile display of soybean meal with one tick scale.

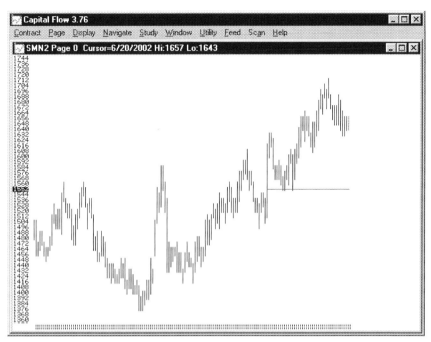

Figure 11–15 Daily bar of soybean meal with buy signal generated from single prints and neutral day indicated by horizontal line.

Provided by Steidlmayer Software Inc.

ods) encompassing the total day's range less a tick either side of the first hour's range. The new high by a tick in the "H" period and a new low by a tick in the "J" period is by definition an old-fashioned symmetrical neutral day. This neutral day, or change day, trades halfway back into the single prints or minus development of the composite profile (referenced by the horizontal line). In summary, the background is positive, the foreground is projecting higher prices, pull the trigger, put on the trade. Figure 11–15 displays the fruits of your labor. The horizontal line originating from the large vertical bar is referencing the minus development (single prints) from the composite profile, the entry price for your trade. The ensuing price activity saw the market rally from 15.60 to approximately 17.00, a $1,400 profit on a one lot.

Moving to still a higher level of complexity, a system might include the third page 2 mark back (trend indicator), confirming directional arrow generated from the market activity display in Capflow32, and one-dimensionality within volume dollars confirmed by holding the zero line. (These studies will be covered in Chapter 13.)

As you can see, the system a trader creates is limited only by the tools at her or his disposal, her or his market understanding and personal creativity. Do be aware that the more filters you integrate to create a system, the fewer signals will be generated. For instance, if you are using the filter of single prints as your trigger, you may find a trade a day. If you add the filter of volume dollars to confirm the direction, your trade frequency may fall to three trades per week. Adding still another filter of the third page 2 mark back indicating trend with volume confirmation and minus development generated by single prints, trade frequency may fall to one trade or fewer per week.

Creating a more comprehensive signal will decrease trade frequency and hopefully improve your winning percentage as well as profits. Ideally, that should be the goal of any trading program. The downside to creating systems with decreased trade frequency is idle cash sitting in your trading account. To overcome this problem, I suggest overlaying your systematic approach to a diversified portfolio of contracts. This should offer diversification as well as smooth out your equity curve.

Chapter 12

PROFILE OF THE SUCCESSFUL TRADER

Trading is being young, imperfect, and human—not old, exacting, and scientific. It is not a set of techniques, but a commitment. You are to be an information processor. Not a swami. Not a guru. An information processor.

Participating in the markets can only develop your trading skills. You need to become a part of the markets, to know the state of the markets at any given time, and most importantly, to know yourself. You need to be patient, confident, and mentally tough.

Good traders offer no excuses, make no complaints. They live willingly with the vagaries of life and the markets.

Start by becoming capital-safe, so that you can participate in the markets on an ongoing basis. Position yourself so that you cannot be knocked out of a market by a few setbacks. Continuous involvement prepares you to take advantage of any good opportunity that arises. It also contributes to your self-confidence. It creates a safe environment in which you can experiment and learn, knowing that no experience will be a career-ending one.

As your trading experience grows, you will begin to gain a feel for the market that enables you to sense changes as they occur, not after. You will develop the ability to recognize opportunities rather than going after dreamed-up trades. You will learn to recognize when you are wrong before your dollar position tells you so. And you will begin to see that, when you have exited a trade, it was usually the right thing to do. In other words, you will begin to experience trading. You become one with the market.

Now it is time to further sharpen and refine your skills—to work to learn. Try to develop a sense of the price/value relationship underlying the trades you make. You will find that there are only three possible price/value relationships: at value, above value, or below value. If your trades are not buying prices above value and selling a prices below value, your trading circumstances will be favorable; the effect of your mistakes will be muted, and it will be relatively easy to recover from them. Mistakes outside these parameters can be disastrous and career-ending.

In the early stages of your trading career, pay attention not only to whether you should buy or sell but also to how you have executed your trading ideas. You will learn more from your trades this way.

Never assume that the unreasonable or the unexpected cannot happen. It can. It does. It will.

Remember, you can learn a lot about trading from your mistakes. When you make a mistake—and you will—do not dwell on the negatives. Learn from the mistake and keep going.

Never forget that markets are made up of people. Think constantly about what others are doing, what they might do in the current circumstances, or what they might do when those circumstances change. Remember that, whenever you buy and hope to sell higher, the person you sell to will have to see the same opportunity at that higher price to be induced to buy.

You will need a sound approach—one that allows you to win at trading. It is best to try to win on the grind. Plan on taking a small profit from a large number of trades, as well as a large profit from a small number of trades.

Traders who lose follow one of several typical patterns. Some repeatedly suffer individual large losses that wipe out earlier gains or greatly increase a small loss. Others experience brief periods during which their trading wheels fall off: they lose discipline and control and make a series of bad trades as a result.

Wise traders make many small trades, remain involved, and constantly maintain and sharpen their feel for the market. For all of their work, they hope to receive some profit, even if it is small in terms of dollars. In addition, continual participation allows them to sense and recognize the few real opportunities when they arise. These generate large rewards that make the effort of trading truly worthwhile.

Do not use arbitrary "monetary stops" when exiting a trade. In other words, do not buy a stock at $40/share and arbitrarily place a sell stop at $36 with the intent of risking a 10 percent move in the underlying. Instead, you should study the trade setup and choose an exit price dictated by market activity. For example, reading market activity may indicate the location of the exit price should be at $37.50 or possibly $32.00. You may be comfortable with a stop at $37.50, but you may wave off the trade with a stop at $32.00 because you cannot justify risking a 20 percent move in the stock. Simply stated, plan your trade before you execute. And trade your plan after you execute.

Now I would like to share a few more specific observations that have a high enough probability of reoccurring that you can almost consider them rules:

1. If you find yourself holding a winning position, adding up your profits, and confidently projecting larger gains on the horizon, you are probably better off exiting the trade. The odds are that the trade has run its course.
2. When entering a trade with a market order and your fill is clearly better than expected, odds are it will end up being a losing trade. Good fill, bad trade. Get out!
3. If all your "trading buddies" agree with your expectations regarding the next big move, it probably will not work out. If everyone's conviction level is as strong as the consensus, do the opposite.

Chapter 13

TRADING, TECHNOLOGY, AND THE FUTURE

In its most pure form, trading allows money to be made in two ways: via content and via access. Trading an opportunity versus getting the edge. Some would argue there is actually a third: having pockets deep enough to afford one the staying power to sit through adverse price movements until the idea finally wins out. This should not be seen as an option because there is always "a trade out there with your name on it" and if you approach the market from this perspective, "it will get you".

Long-term Capital

A great example of staying with a losing position and having it blow up in your face was the Long-term Capital debacle that took place during the fall of 1998. For those not familiar with the story, I provide a thumbnail sketch. Nobel Prize recipients join forces with Wall Street trading gurus, setting up a hedge fund to trade fixed income and foreign exchange markets. They develop proprietary models that incorporated interest rates, stock market levels, currency values, and pattern recognition (just to name a few) in an attempt to find trade opportunities. Based on these models, they placed bets on the market. For many years Long-term Capital did very well with their program, and it brought them a great deal of recognition and trading capital. They always seemed to outperform their benchmark, if for no other reason than they traded with greater leverage. Problem: trading with leverage is a double-edged sword, it is great when you are right but can really hurt you if you are wrong.

There is a saying, "don't turn a mistake into a problem"; in other words, do not attempt to manage bad trades into breakeven or winners, just get out and start fresh. You will expend all your energy and go through all kinds of mental gymnastics trying to break even.

Long-term Capital did not practice this. Whether they believed they were bigger than the market (their order flow could dictate direction), smarter than the market (they were right and everyone else was wrong) or just stubborn, I do not know. But the mismanagement of their portfolio almost brought down the financial infrastructure of the Western world. If it were not for Alan Greenspan and Robert Rubin spearheading a bailout of Long-term Capital by the financial community, the investment landscape as we know it today would be much different. Long-term Capital did not put themselves in a position to lose a battle but win a war—they tried to win the war at all costs. They did not control their risk. Whether you are a fund manager or individual trader/investor, some lessons should be learned from what transpired with Long-term Capital.

Market Profile Display

Let us get back to the focus of this chapter, which is the ways to make money trading. We said the two ways to make money are with content and with access. We define content as generating a trading idea. We define access as order routing and the fill. Up to this point, our entire focus has been on content, with Market Profile as our organizational tool. We have gone to great lengths to educate the reader on how to organize and read a Market Profile display. Understanding the display should put the reader in a position to make money and continue to grow. Grow through trading experiences and grow through ongoing education. From growth comes opportunity. An emerging market offers many more opportunities than a mature market. It offers less competition, higher margins, and more upside. Contrast that with a mature market that has more competition, tighter margins, and less upside. From a philosophical standpoint, ask yourself these questions: on reaching a fork in the road, do you choose the road less traveled or do you prefer the clearly marked trail? The explored or the unexplored? The known or the unknown? Generally the more difficult, less secure option has a bigger payoff at the end.

Thinking outside the box and staying ahead of the curve are how you succeed in a growth industry. The likes of Henry Ford, Bill Gates, and Michael Dell did not sit idly and watch competition and technology pass them by. They forged ahead to improve and expand on their ideas. As the developers of Market Profile, we could have stayed where we were with the original methodology and fought to gain market share in a maturing market. Instead, we retooled ourselves. We opted to go the growth route. We have done this with the development of the Capital Flow software products. Figure 13–1 illustrates what I call the Market Profile flow chart pyramid, which gives a

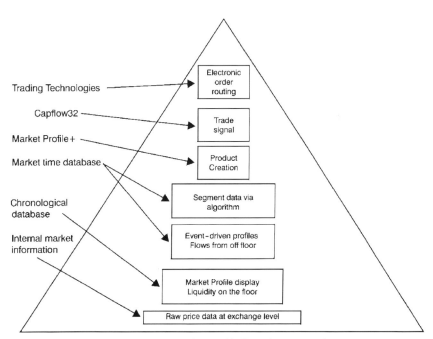

Figure 13–1   Market Profile flow chart pyramid.

chronological representation of the evolution we have gone through with the Market Profile. Every aspect of the development is not chronicled; we have chosen to list only the most salient points. Conceptually, the word pyramid seemed a logical display to convey this idea. The base or foundation of the pyramid needs to be strong to support the massive weight of the structure. The base or foundation of our methodology is the bell curve, the building blocks of Market Profile. As we move from this stable base to the apex of the pyramid, computer processing and technology become more integrated into the process. Our philosophy has always been to keep forging ahead, to utilize our intellectual capital. The result of these efforts is the Market Profile flow chart pyramid.

Now let us go to work explaining the diagram. At the base are the raw price data generated at the exchange level. Price data are internal to the market, a byproduct of participant trading, a commodity. In their raw form, price data have limited value; processed, their value is greatly increased. We call this the uplift process and you see it all around you. Processed wheat becomes bread and processed mold becomes penicillin. We have a saying, "make price the messenger, not the message." Price is an "unfinished good"; it needs to be processed to make it more "palatable," more valuable.

The Market Profile display is our answer to processed data for the trading community. Figure 13–2 is a daily Market Profile display of March copper. The screen display has been compressed to show more data. The Market Profile display takes raw price data from any stock or commodity exchange and puts them into an easily readable value-added format for the end-user. As a trader, you move away from being a "tape reader" to using an organizational tool to help interpret price activity. Not to say tape readers have not been successful—Jesse Livermore is one of the most famous—but we need to integrate the latest technology and ideas to improve our system. Just because something works does not mean you cannot make it better. Thus, the second tier of our pyramid, the Market Profile display, is an organizational tool we have developed that lets the user create a two-dimensional (vertical and horizontal) database.

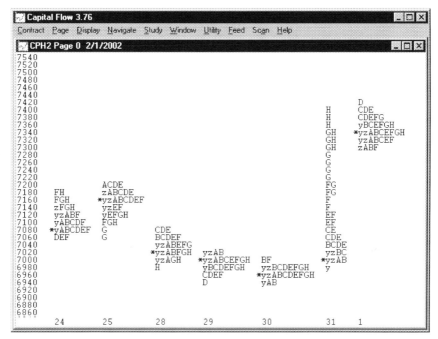

Figure 13–2   Daily Market Profile display of March copper.

Copyright © 1984 Chicago Board of Trade. All Rights Reserved. CBOT Market Profile, Market Profile, Liquidity Data Bank, and LDB are registered trademarks of the Chicago Board of Trade. All Rights Reserved. Provided by Steidlmayer Software Inc.

Market Time

The limiting factor of the Market Profile was the segmentation process that created a chronological profile. Early on, this limitation did not exist because most trading was confined to a single day; participants would square up at the end of the day and start the whole process over again the next day. However with the advent of funds and 24-hour markets, we needed to find ways to organize data beyond the industry standard, which is a chronological format. From that realization came Steidlmayer Softwares' first product, Capital Flow 3.7. Within this platform, the user has the ability to create what we call a market time database. Figure 13–3 shows the same information as in Figure 13–2 but in a dif-

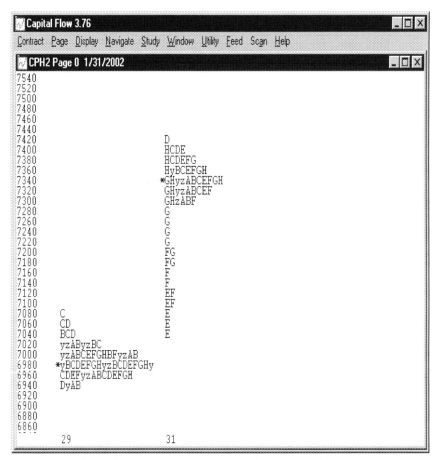

Figure 13–3   Market time database display of March copper.

ferent format. We combine the sideways days to make a longer duration 3:1:3, which is segmented from the existing distribution (3:2:1 up) when the market finally makes up its mind to rally. The standard Market Profile (see Fig. 13–2) is superior to any other type of display available in the industry, yet it still has its limitations in that it organizes data in a chronological format (daily Market Profile). Moving the organization and display to a market time database (see Fig. 13–3) gives the user an entirely different perspective of the market, one that is reflective of market movement as opposed to one that is a function of some arbitrary time interval. A chronological profile is dynamic in that both the horizontal and the vertical dimensions can grow. However, it has an arbitrary shutoff point (the close) that doesn't allow for the "entire picture" to be painted. The creation of a market time database allows for the entire picture to be painted and signed before the artist starts the next work. This picture or event is dependent on where the user begins the structure, which is a function of her or his time frame and understanding of the markets. From a charting standpoint, the events (price movement) represent the four steps of market activity discussed in Chapter 6. What constitutes an event is a function of the time frame the participant is monitoring. A relatively insignificant event (price movement) will appear on the radar screen of someone trading a short-term time frame; however, the same price movement is nothing more than noise for the longer–time frame participant. Thus, segmenting a daily profile into something less than a daily or combining daily profiles to create a composite profile is a function of the time frame the user is trading. Of course, there are times you realize your "picture" is actually part of a much larger "mural" or that you could have painted a clearer picture; however, this comes with time if you apply yourself.

Auto Splitter

The single greatest limitation to working the data manually (looking at each individual contract and telling the computer where to segment) is time, the one thing none of us seem to have enough of. To address this need, we had the first major upgrade to the software, which was the patented auto splitter. Figure 13–4 contains the same data as displayed in the previous two charts (March copper over 6 or 7 days), but it is segmented with the auto splitter. Along the bottom of the page, the dates are duplicated, meaning each daily profile is segmented into many smaller profiles. The number of times within the day the profile is segmented varies and is a function of the horizontal/vertical relationship of the given instrument and how the algorithm is

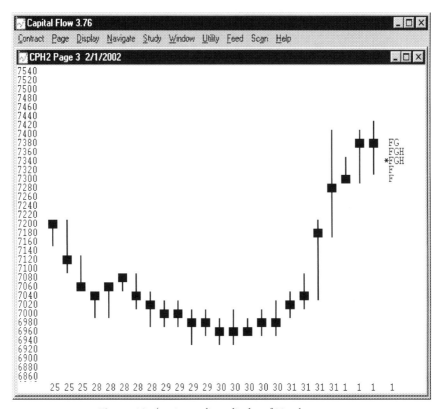

Figure 13–4 Auto splitter display of March copper.

set. This moved the segmentation process out of the hands of the user and into the computer, via an algorithm. A trader was finally able to get around the horn (look at multiple markets in a timely fashion).

At about the same time we created the auto splitter functionality, we shifted our visual presentation model to a foreground-, background-type display. When generating a trading idea, you want to look at dissimilar information that generates similar output and that should serve as confirmation of an opportunity. This is accomplished by looking at different time frames. Earlier, we defined the minimum trend as the smallest working part of the market. It is a mini-distribution, micro 3:2:1 structure, kind of like a high-resolution TV, giving you a very clear picture of the market. We call this short-term perspective the foreground. Using the same auto splitter technology with a different algorithm, we are able to create larger profiles. The concept of looking for distributions is the same as before, the only difference is we are looking for "larger" distributions. We call this our background perspective. Those familiar with current Market Profile vernacular would know this as page2 information. Maintaining the continuity of our example, Figure 13–5

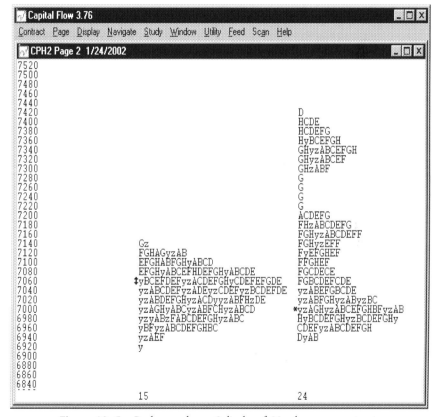

Figure 13–5 Background, page2 display of March copper contract.

again is the March copper contract. The main difference of this page2 display is that we are combining days to create a larger profile as opposed to segmenting a daily profile into smaller units.

Focused Output

To avoid the need to jump back and forth between pages, we superimposed the relevant information from the background page (page2) over the foreground page to create focused output. Figure 13–6 displays the focused output of the March copper contract. The vertical lines with the little black boxes attached are the 7 days of price activity segmented into their smallest working part via the auto splitter. The little black boxes are called the control price for the unit; they signify the anchor for the unit they are attached to or, more importantly, the starting point of the follow-

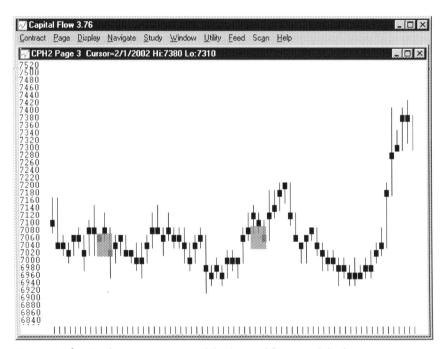

Figure 13–6 March copper contract with background/foreground display.
Provided by Steidlmayer Software Inc.

ing unit's distribution or micro money flow. The two larger, lighter-colored boxes are the control prices for the two macro profiles we built and displayed as Figure 13–5. The interpretation of the larger boxes (page2 marks) is the same as the control price, which is the anchor for the developed profile and the distribution point for the new price activity. Our unique database of market time information is what sets us apart from the rest of the industry. We are not trading a daily bar only to realize we should be trading the weekly perspective or trading the hourly only to realize we should be trading the 30-minute. No, first of all this is chronological, external information that randomly overlays a subjective time interval. Instead, we are creating a market time database that communicates what is going on in the market place.

Proprietary Studies

Not only is our database unique but the studies that overlay it are also unique to the industry. There are pipe studies that "compress" data and allow for more information to be displayed in a limited amount of space. There are design management ratio (DMR) studies that project stopping levels based on handicapping initial price movement. Figure 13–7 is a Steidlmayer bar chart of Intel Corporation with a DMR overlay. Note the large box and the smaller box in its lower left-hand corner. There are also two numbers above the upper left-hand corner of the larger and smaller boxes. The DMR projects price probes as potential stopping areas (in four steps of market activity) based on a handicapping formula generated from the first two units of price activity coming out of some price control zone. In the lower left-hand corner of the large box, the smaller box encapsulates two units with a set of numbers above it. The lower number of the two represents an actual ratio based on the horizontal/vertical relationship of the two bars. The upper number of the set is the result of a formula developed to help handicap the price burst out of price control. As we continue to recalculate this study and new price data come into the database, the actual ratio and handicapped ratio numbers begin to converge until they reach a point in time when

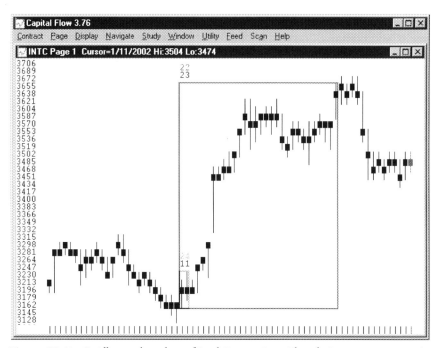

Figure 13–7   Steidlmayer bar chart of Intel Corporation with a design management ratio (DMR).

Provided by Steidlmayer Software Inc.

they are equal to or within 10 percent of each other. When these numbers reach this point of convergence, the market is telling us the distribution phase should be moving to the stopping and development phase of the four steps of Market Activity. Signaling the stopping could be a function of the vertical expanding, the horizontal growing, or a combination of the two. Most importantly, we are not trying to predict the future, but to process data based on the vertical/horizontal relationship in an attempt to determine when the market may be moving to the stopping phase. In our example, we started with an actual ratio of 11 and a handicapped ratio of 24. We added more data until the actual ratio became 23 and the handicapped or DMR became 22. At that point when the two numbers converge, the market should at least take a breath and trade sideways or possibly reverse the directional move being measured.

There are compression studies which display the first or first and second standard deviations of a defined amount of data. Figure 13–8 displays a compression study overlaying a defined amount of data for the March Canadian dollar futures contract. If this bar chart were displayed in a profile format, it would be some form of a 3:2:1 up with the preponderance of time/price opportunities (TPOs) (letters) in the upper third of the unit's range. The relevant information for the compression study is displayed above the compression box in the left-hand corner. For this example, we have chosen to display a compression study of 68 percent of the TPO data. Whenever you see any form of a 3:2:1, the first standard deviation or 68 percent of the data should be the selected option. Whenever you see a 3:1:3 structure, locate the first and second standard deviations or select 95 percent of the data. Looking at Figure 13–8, you can see that 68 percent of the data over this sample is displayed as the shaded area within the box.

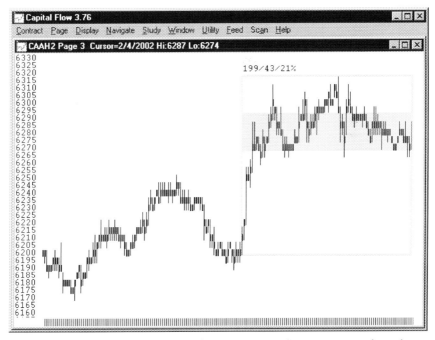

Figure 13–8　March Canadian dollar futures contract with compression study overlay. Provided by Steidlmayer Software Inc.

In addition, there are three numbers below the compression study percentage—those numbers being 199/43/21%. The first number (199) represents the number of half-hour bars over the sample. The middle number (43) records the number of times the mode (event with highest frequency of recurrence) traded over the sample. The percentage number (21%) indicates the percentage of the mode (43) relative to the total sample (199). In other words, the mode traded in 21% of the 199 bars, or 43 bars in total. The compression studies are useful in defining where value is for a structure. The 68 percent compression is displaying the stopping and development areas in the four steps of market activity. Finding a 3:1:3 structure and setting a 95 percent compression study will show the outer boundaries of price control for an efficient market. If you believe the market is going to remain efficient or contained within the existing development, you can buy toward the bottom of the compression and sell toward the top of the compression.

Lonesome Dove/Other Studies

The lonesome dove calculation is similar to that of the strange attractor, which you may have read about in chaos theory. The concept being that short-term, the market moves away from it; longer-term, it gravitates back toward it. Vertical ratio studies measure momentum. Horizontal ratio studies assist the user in determining where current development falls within the four steps of market activity. By no means is this list meant to be exhaustive; its sole purpose is to give the reader a taste for what is available in the system. These proprietary studies to Capital Flow software all have one thing in common—they use the processing power of the computer. In fact, all the applications toward the top of the Market Profile flow chart pyramid possess this trait.

Product Creation

Moving further up the Market Profile flow chart pyramid, we come to product creation. Product creation is a function of using

Market Profile+, which is available in Capflow32 and other third-party vendors. Market Profile+ applies the uplift process to the original Market Profile, utilizing the segmentation algorithm described earlier, and combines contracts that have no economic relationship to create a traded instrument that we call a product.

Trading at its core is confrontational but product creation is usage; thus, the benefit of trading a product over a contract. By confrontational, we mean there is a winner for every loser (this has been described as the zero sum game in game theory). This can be true only when participants are trading the same time frame and trading nothing else against that position. In the real world, participants are trading different time frames, which is why the process of trading is not self-defeating. When combining different underlying contracts to make a product, the traders' goal is to create cash flow. This product mix could be a combination of long and short positions in unrelated instruments. The mix could include any stock or commodity that has liquidity. Figure 13–9 is a screen display from Capflow32 of a created product whose components are the 5-year note, mini Standard and Poor (S&P), Euro currency, soybeans, and IBM stock. On the contract line are a listing of the components, their weighting, and directional bias (long or short). Once you input this information, a Market Profile display can be created for the product. Each profile in the display is predominantly black with patches of color in some profiles. The black in the profile represents the standard or normal range of prices for the composite or product that has been created. When creating the product, each component is assigned a color, and when a component moves beyond its norm, the part of the profile representing the aberration is color-coded for the component creating that volatility. Because we are not using color examples, it is hard to tell which component is influencing price movement beyond the norm; but if you look closely, you can see shades of gray in some profiles. If we had a color display, we could see specifically which component (5-year, mini S&P, Euro currency, soy beans, or IBM) was influencing price movement beyond the norm, causing the shade of gray.

Once again, the purpose for creating a product is to generate cash flow. We have accomplished our goal in the example be-

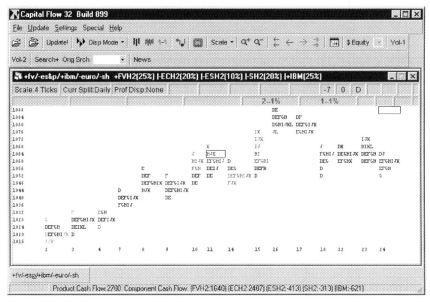

Figure 13–9 Five-year note, Mini Standard and Poor, Euro currency, soybeans, and IBM stock combined to make a product.

Provided by Steidlmayer Software Inc.

cause the right-most profile (most recent) is at a higher price than the left-most profile (oldest). In other words, the net cash flow of being long the 5-year at 25 percent, short the Euro currency at 20 percent, short the mini S&P at 10 percent, short the soybeans at 20 percent, and long IBM at 25 percent generated positive cash flow of 2780. This information is displayed at the bottom of the screen along with the performance of each individual leg of the product.

By combining these different instruments, you are bringing the portfolio effect into play. Creating the diversification all investment advisors advocate. Once the product stops generating positive cash flow, the trader has two options: tweak the mix (get out of the contract that is negatively affecting cash flow and into another) or liquidate the trade and start over. In this example, you can see the components' performance at the bottom of the page. You may want to tweak the mix by dropping the biggest loser (long IBM is down 621), or you may feel that the strongest component has run its course (short Euro currency is up 2487), so you dump it and add something else. Another option is to dump the product entirely and create a new one.

Capflow32

Referencing back to our pyramid, the height of complexity from a processed trade standpoint lies in the signal generation capabilities of Capflow32. This processing revolution that has taken place over the last 10 years is totally mind-boggling. It is like morphing forward in time from the ice age to the 20th century. Not too long ago, programs were run on punched cards and mainframes. Today, you have more processing power on your desktop than you had in a room full of computers 20 years ago. With this added processing power, we are able to generate signals that are a totally objective read of market activity. From the segmentation algorithm, which is a user-defined parameter, to the combining of indicators that generate the trade signal, users are in the "cockpit" creating a system unique to themselves—their own black box. The system could be price-based, volume-based, or a combination of the two. Profiles can be coded based on the degree of horizontal to create Market Activity Units and their byproduct of directional arrows. Figure 13–10 is a market activity display of AT&T with the system-generated directional arrow displayed. The arrow is derived from the coding of the Market Profiles as extreme price control, price control, non–price control, or trending and the sequencing of the profiles. To simplify the display, we assign blue, green, and red balls to the extreme price control, price control, and non–price control profiles, respectively; and a vertical line to the trending profiles. In this example based on the coding and sequencing, the system generated a sell signal on January 15 at the price of 18.75. In just over a month's time, the stock was trading at 14.25, a 25 percent break.

Other applications or studies available in Capflow32 include longevity dates, which are calculated to show the duration of any directional move. The Helix can be used to assist in interpreting any of the bias information (strong buying, strong selling, weak buying, weak selling) relative to the trend indicator of the

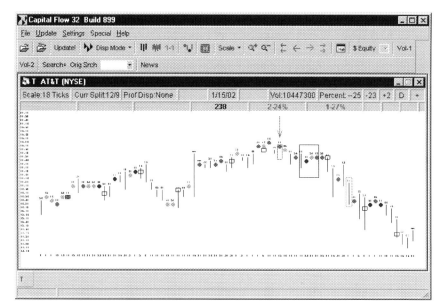

Figure 13–10   Market activity display of AT&T with directional arrow.
Provided by Steidlmayer Software Inc.

third page2 mark back. Moving onto volume, any of the volume studies covered in Chapter 7 can be built into a system and traded. Volume is the "footprint" the market leaves in its wake; picking up on heavy volume, light volume, and volume excesses communicates a great deal of information to the trader. Once again, this short list of applications is not meant to be exhaustive; its purpose is to give the reader a flavor of what is available and can be automated in Capflow32.

Remember the two ways to make money in trading are recognizing opportunities and getting the edge. Up to this point, our entire focus has been on understanding and applying the Market Profile methodology to finding trading opportunities. It is a necessary process one needs to go through to become successful. You need to go to school and pay your tuition and study your lessons before you can go out into the real world and attempt to make a living.

The second way to make money in trading is a bit more straightforward, is more interactive, and has a shorter learning curve. It is a function of using the latest technology and best product. This is the model used by a well-known options trading group to make Chicago synonymous with options and put the city on the trading map. Their name was Chicago Research and Trading (CRT). They attempted to be part of every trade with their cutting edge technology and traders populating every pit (access). They were looking for the edge. They were creating a low-margin business, the grocery store model of high-volume, low-markup. They were the first to commit to this model in such a grand scale, and as in anything in life, it pays to be first with a good idea.

What is Access?

Access means different things to different people. At its core, it is getting an order to the exchange. This can be accomplished by talking to your broker, being on the floor, or using electronic order entry. In the investment world, technology has probably affected access more than any other facet of the business.

This revolution has taken place over the last 10 years and really came to a head over the past 2 years. Let us use the access flow chart pyramid in Figure 13–11 to illustrate this point.

At the base of the pyramid, we see raw price data at the exchange level followed by connectivity to exchange. Earlier, we listed raw price data and the broadcast of that information as a commodity just as electronic access would have been considered a commodity early in its existence. By saying electronic access is a commodity I mean all front-end providers offered essentially the same utility with the same limitations. In the access flow chart pyramid, the next level is "price display on front-end." This price display, which we call the first generation of electronic order entry, was keyboard-driven, clumsy, and unique to each exchange. The next generation brought front-end providers that accessed multiple exchanges with point and click technology. During the time of commoditization of order routing, the only thing that set the order routing firms apart was their logo on the splash screen. However, during the last 2 years, these providers have attempted to differentiate themselves by offering

Figure 13–11   Access flow chart pyramid.

different bells and whistles, creating the "x" generation of electronic order routing.

Looking at front-end providers, the common denominators to use for comparison purposes are speed of access and reliability. How long does it take to get an order from your desktop to the exchange? How much downtime does the system experience? In reality, speed is a function of the desktop layout, coding, technology, and routing. A person looking intently at the order routing screen takes between 80 and 130 milliseconds to react to price change, volume info, news blips, and so on. The big attraction to trade electronic exchanges lies in the level playing field offered to all participants. By that I mean once the order reaches the exchange, it is processed and queued by the standard accounting practice of *fifo* (first in, first out). It does not matter who you are or who you know, if your order is first to the exchange you will get filled first. Therefore, if a trader hesitates for an instance because she or he is not confident, her or his mouse is positioned over the correct price, volume numbers need to be accumulated, or she or he needs to focus on another screen to get some relevant information, the trade could be gone or the trade price could be significantly different.

MD_Trader

Trading Technologies' (TT's) X_TRADER® with the MD_Trader™ display presents prices with accumulated volume traded at a price in a patent pending static vertical price display. (X_TRADER® is a registered trademark and MD_Trader™ is a trademark of Trading Technologies International, Inc., of Chicago, Illinois). In the display, consecutive prices in a price array are displayed in a static vertical format, with changing bids and offers denoted in columns to the left and right, respectively, of the static vertical price column. Figure 13–12 is an

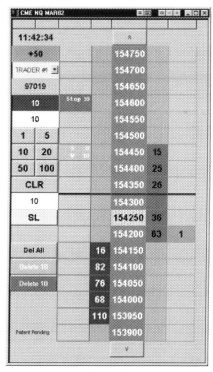

Figure 13–12   MD_Trader™ display of the Mini Nasdaq.

MD_Trader™ display of the Mini Nasdaq. On the left-most side of the display are the components needed to enter trade size, account number, and other relevant information. In the next column to the right, all your working orders are denoted. Farther to the right is the price array for the underlying instrument with the book (existing bids below and offers above). The last column lists the price and quantity for the last trade. This superior format—and we know it is superior because all the competitors are attempting to copy it—has a consolidation feature that allows for more or fewer prices to be displayed in the MD_Trader™ display. This feature comes in handy during periods of extreme volatility (e.g., release of economic numbers, news events). Combining all these features elevates your confidence level in responding and clicking the price you want to be trading. Another feature of the MD_Trader™ is center clicking, which positions the currently traded price to the center of the MD_Trader™ display window. Therefore, from a pure speed perspective, TT's X_TRADER® front end with the MD_Trader™ display provides what you are looking for, the fastest access to the market.

Two satisfied customers have had this to say about the product: D.J. Martin, independent trader with an MBA from New York University (NYU), whose dream was to move to Chicago and strike it rich as a trader. He moved to Chicago during the summer of 1997. Over the next 4 years, D.J. came close to losing his nest egg more times than he cares to remember; however, he always managed to fight back and make enough to live on. He realized there was something missing in his trading, so he made the change to TT during the summer of 2001. Since switching to TT, he has not had a losing week, has had 6 straight winning months, and has strung together 94 winning days in a row. "Since I started using TT, my income has increased by almost $600,000 a year. My trading approach has remained the same; therefore, I must conclude my recent success is directly related to using MD_Trader™ and other innovative tools and cutting edge technology offered at TT." This from Chuck McElveen, owner/operator Kingstree Trading, a large Chicago-based proprietary trading firm that accounts for the largest percentage of daily mini volume traded at the Chicago Mercantile Exchange (CME). "Since opening our doors, TT has been our company-wide solution for trading software. Without question, we could not have achieved the same success or traded as much volume without MD_Trader™. No other application allows you to fully capture the flow of the market and to capitalize on that flow with speed and precision. Our relationship with TT goes back to the company's inception, so it's difficult to assign a dollar amount or percentage by which they have contributed to the bottom line. I can say, however, that having my traders use TT front-end has positively impacted profitability at Kingstree Trading." With speed being our basis of comparison, TT has the others beat hands-down. The process is faster and more reliable.

The next layer of comparison is looking at what front-end providers have done to differentiate themselves from a value-added perspective. This is where TT has really distinguished themselves. They have created automated order execution and management tools. At this point in time, the application that really sets TT apart from the rest of the competition is the Autospreader. The Autospreader allows for the entry of two-legged spreads with a high degree of reliability. The key word here is reliability; it is one thing to offer the functionality, yet another to deliver. There is no worse feeling than entering a spread order, getting hit on one leg, and subsequently watching the market move sharply against you. The Autospreader allows the trader to set up a spread and enter spread orders in an MD_Trader™ display. After an order is entered, the tool automatically enters orders into the outright legs and manages those orders. The Autospreader automatically sends offset orders into the other leg once an order in one leg has been filled.

Figure 13–13 is a screen capture of the Autospreader with the corresponding underlying futures contracts. The Autospreader is the leftmost MD_Trader™ display, and the futures contracts are the right two MD_Trader™ displays. In setting up the spread ma-

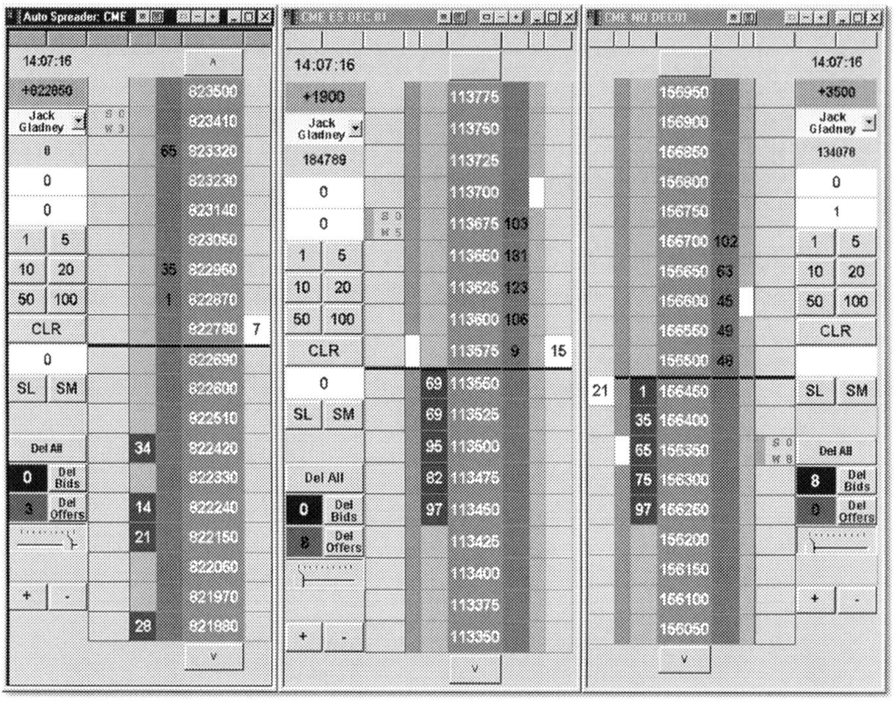

Figure 13–13   Autospreader with corresponding underlying futures contracts.

trix, the creator inputs the bias, weighting, price display prefer-
ence, fudge factor, and a number of other user-defined parameters that control how the spread order is entered and managed. In
setting up your spread template, each spread is color-coded and
that color is used to enter orders in the MD_Trader™ display so
the trader can differentiate between outright and spread orders.
Once the spread order is entered into the Autospreader, the components are entered and modified with the changes in the underlying to maintain the inputted spread relationship. You can
see the spread order in the Autospreader and the corresponding
bid and offer in the Mini S&P and Mini Nasdaq.

TT is also working on another automated order execu-
tion/management tool that is due to be available shortly after
the publication of this book. This automated order execution
tool, to be called Autotrader, is an order routing application that

can be used by systems traders to trade their black box. For example, any single indicator or group of contingency signals can be routed through a TT front-end and executed. Multiple account management and embedded formulas are accepted by the system, making this feature useful for the managed funds industry. Autotrader will be a utility within X_TRADER® allowing for system-generated signals to be executed via an Excel or Visual Basic (VB) link. Autotrader will list contracts traded within the system, account numbers, open positions, current bid/ask market, and working orders. As the mix of contracts traded in your system becomes larger or smaller, the Autotrader window can be sized accordingly.

Recall the apex of the Market Profile flow chart pyramid is automated signal generation and execution of those signals. The apex of the access flow chart pyramid is point and click technology in order entry, which we has been automated with tools such as TT's Autospreader and Autotrader. The apex of our pyramid (the traders) is moving our energies to management of trades and away from being an observer. Make the computer the observer, let it process information based on our ideas, systematize those ideas, and then objectively generate signals off those ideas.

An Excel application can be used by third-party vendors to display their proprietary indicators in the MD_Trader™ display. Proprietary indicators such as volume excesses, page2 marks, bias indicators, and directional arrows generated by the likes of Capflow32 can be color coded and displayed as markers in the MD_Trader™ display in dynamic indicator columns to the left or right of the static price array. This focused output is the result of a system running in the background and updating the order routing system with relevant processed data. Figure 13–14 is an MD_Trader™ display of the Mini Nasdaq with that additional column to the left or right of the book bid and offer columns, respectively. We have created our markers in this example off a link to Capflow32 referencing page2 marks and directional arrows. For display purposes, we have color-coded the markers white and off-white. Copying levels or signals into the dynamic indicator columns of the MD_Trader™ display serves two purposes: getting information to you in a timely fashion and eliminating the need to jockey back and forth between systems.

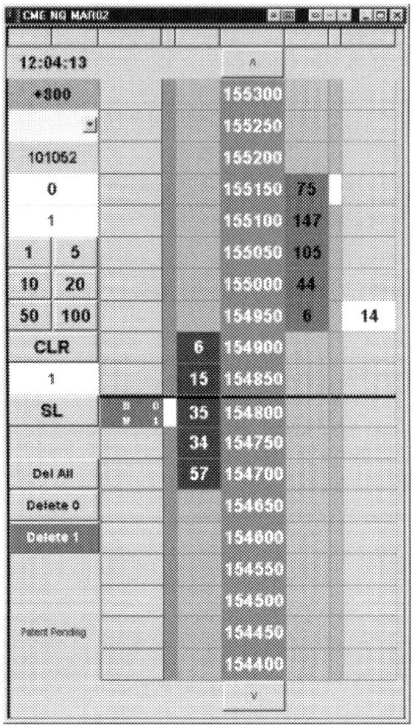

Figure 13–14 MD_Trader™ display of Mini Nasdaq with additional column for markers.

The innovation pipeline at TT is always open, working on making a better product for the professional trader. And who will be helping to stoke that pipeline? None other than Harris Brumfield—trader, innovator, and visionary. Whether it be in the controlled chaos of the Treasury bond pit at the CBOT or sitting behind a screen trading electronically, Harris Brumfield has always been a force to reckon with. While he was still one of the largest locals trading on the floor, Harris began his transition to upstairs trading in 1998. Why make the change? Because the screen could accommodate his size better than the floor. His experiences and success on the floor soon made him realize something was missing in the existing screen-based displays. That started a relationship with TT that still exists today. First, he contracted with TT to develop some of his ideas concerning screen display. The process went through many iterations and the end result was MD_Trader™. By the time this came to fruition, Harris was the largest shareholder in the privately held company. In addition to the MD_Trader™, Harris is credited with developing the one-sided trading card, which is used on many open outcry exchanges. Owing to these innovations and others, his peers have called him a visionary. Rest assured that this creative genius will continue to hone his wares, keeping TT at the head of the pack in electronic order entry.

By running Capflow32 parallel to the TT front-end, the trader has turned his or her desktop into a virtual exchange. With a desktop exchange, the limitations fall squarely on the shoulders of the user and his or her creativity or lack thereof. Your business resides on your desktop and consists of connectivity, order routing, and content. From there an empire can be built.

Other Access Options

Now let us try to determine what is the best form of access. Remember, there are basically three forms of access: floor, electronic, and phone. Phone immediately falls to the bottom of the list owing to cost, delays in getting orders entered, delays in fill confirmation, and communication errors. On an electronic platform, the cost of trading is substantially less than the standard phone access but more costly than trading directly on the floor. On the flip side on the coin, cost of floor access (owning or leasing a seat) is more costly than licensing a front-end. In fact, the expense of a clerk is more than the licensing fee of the front-end. The advantage is really shifted to electronic order entry when you look at diversity of access offered by the electronic platform versus the limitations of trading on the floor and narrowing your focus to trading in just one pit. When markets are moving with liquidity, there is not a better place to be than on the floor; however, when volatility comes in and volume dries up, floor traders do things solely for financial reasons—in other words, trading a larger and larger unit to make the daily nut. Our double-edged sword cuts once again because trading with leverage (larger and larger unit) is great when you are right but can be a killer when you are wrong.

Contrast that with trading multiple exchanges, looking over a spectrum of markets, finding the best opportunity, and the choice should be simple. The clear choice is trading opportunities off the floor with electronic access.

Earlier, we touched on a hedge fund going belly up and the possible causes of this. Whether it is lack of discipline, operator error (incorrectly entering quantity or direction), or miscalculating position or risk of position, all of these potential problems are addressed with the risk management software offered by TT called X_RISK™. This should be a comforting thought for all parties involved: the investor, the clearinghouse, and the trader. Open positions are tracked mark to market with a running profit and loss. The clearinghouse sets limits (quantity traded and currency loss amounts) for all accounts. This controls the potential for career-ending mistakes and also the effect a rogue trader can have on a firm.

In this chapter, titled Trading, Technology, and the Future, we have addressed the ways to make money in trading: via content and via access. To close out this chapter, I would like to make an agricultural analogy. In trading, we have defined content as finding an opportunity. From an agricultural standpoint, could we not equate finding a trading opportunity to producing a crop? Second, in trading, we have defined access as the order routing process. From an agricultural standpoint, could we not equate the order routing process to the delivery mechanism for the crop? By that we mean harvesting the crop and getting it to the end-user. Did you know that over the past 10 years, Russia has been a buyer of grains from the United States, South America, and at times, China? This was necessary to support their distressed population. Did you also know that over that same time horizon, Russia has produced some bumper crops. You might ask how could this be, why would they still need to import? The answer is, they might be able to produce the grains but they cannot deliver it to where it is needed. It might be sitting out there in the field, but they do not have the modern machinery needed to harvest the crop in a timely and efficient manner nor do they have the infrastructure to deliver the goods. In fact, when they do get the grains out of the field and loaded into railcars, as much as half the crop is lost owing to an outdated rail system (rusted-out railcars with holes), spoilage, and pilferage along the way. Russia has the content (grains) but not the access (delivery mechanism).

Now let us look at a country like Japan, which also imports grains. Japan is technologically advanced and modern and has a good infrastructure in place. There is a large population to feed and no acreage to produce the needed foodstuff. Japan has access (delivery mechanism) but no content (grains).

Lastly, let us look at the United States, which is a net exporter of grains. This may be a bit of an exaggeration, but it has been said that the United States feeds the world. There is acreage to plant, a climate for growing, technology, and infrastructure needed to produce and deliver the goods. The United States has access and content. Should we as traders not be doing the same thing, looking for a blend of the two (access and content) to make ourselves as self-sufficient as possible?

The last word: I would like to leave you with a quote from Calvin Coolidge (1872–1933).

> *Press on: nothing in the world can take the place of perseverance. Talent will not; nothing is more common than unsuccessful men with talent. Genius will not; unrewarded genius is almost a proverb. Education will not; the world is full of educated derelicts. Persistence and determination alone are omnipotent.*

ENDNOTES

Those wishing to expand their horizons on the material covered in this book may contact the coauthor, Steve Hawkins, at his website, profiletrading.com. This site provides information on:

Steidlmayer Software products
- Capital Flow 3.7
- Capflow32
- Product creation

Trading Technologies
- Order routing
- Trade management
- Risk management
- Systems interface

Education
- Market Profile
- Advanced Market Profile
- Latest developments in Market Profile

Money management and systems development
- Integrating content and access, the total solution
- Black box development

Thank you to Don Jones at Cisco Futures and CQG for allowing the use of their screen displays in the book. For more information on these companies or the services they offer, contact Cisco Futures at Cisco-futures.com or CQG at CQG.com.

INDEX

Note: Tables are indicated by "t" and figures are indicated by "f" following the page number.

Access, 203–205
    electronic order entry and, 212
    forms of, 211
Access flow chart pyramid, 204f, 203–204
American Airlines, Market Profile of, 21–22, 22f
American Express, daily Market Profile of, 160, 160f
AOL Time Warner, Market Profile of, 167–168, 168f
Auction point(s), 85–86, 168–171
    definition of, 169
Auctions, types of, in market, 126–127
Auto splitter, 189–194, 192f
Autospreader, 206–208, 208f
Autotrader, 209

Background, in equilibrium, foreground and, 176
Bar chart display, 79, 82f
Bell curve, 40f, 45f
    basic concept of, 17f, 17–18
    behavior around price and, 20
    drawn, 25, 26f
    order and, 18
Beyond-the-day activity, 82–89

Big barn boss, 155
Blow off extreme, 115–117
    in Gillette stock, 116f, 116–117
Book, stacked, 153
Brumfield, Harris, 210
Buying below value, 90
Buying tail, 83

Capflow32, 201–203
    screen display from, 199, 200f
Capital, Long-term, 185–186
Capital Flow 3.7, 189–191
Caterpillar stock, volume@time output, 106, 107f
Cattle, live, Market Profile of, 170f, 170–171
Chart, as communication system, 56
Charting system, price and market condition and, 44
Chicago Board of Trade, 28, 29, 37
    in 1980s, 43–46
    market information programs at, 44–46
    real-time information and, 45–46
Chicago Research and Trading, 203
Chronological database, utilization of, 158–159
Chronological profiles, 69

Cisco Systems, Market Profile of, 65f, 64–65
Citigroup Incorporated, Market Profile of, 24–25, 25f
Commodities, in 1970s, 39–40
Commodity Trader Identification codes, 97
Commodity traders, 16
  article on, 15
  loss of money by, 19
Commodity trading funds, advent of, 37–40
Composite profile, 177f, 176–177
Compression, 195–197
Compression studies, 197f, 197–198
Content, definition of, 186
Coolidge, Calvin, 213
Copper, daily Market Profile display of, 188, 189f
Crude Light, Market Profile of, 68f, 66–68

Daily bar chart, 92, 93f
  of 30-year Treasury bond, 103, 105f, 111, 112f
  of Mattel Inc., 120, 120f
Database, chronological, utilization of, 158–159
  market time, 189–191, 190f
Day structure(s), five typical patterns of, 59–70, 61f, 62f, 63f, 65f, 66t, 68f, 70f
  purpose of, 59
Day structure trading, 163–168
Deal, successful, both dealers satisfied in, 11–12
Dell, Michael, 187
Dennis, Richard, 159
Developmental phase of market activity, 71
Distribution, 71, 131
  normal, 132, 132f
    versus Steidlmayer distribution, 132–134, 133f
  Steidlmayer. See Steidlmayer distribution

Dow futures, daily bar chart of, 171–172, 173f
  on Chicago Board of Trade, 173–174, 174f
Dow futures contract, 30-minute bar chart of, 51, 52f, 53
  graphed to standard Market Profile criteria, 54f, 52–53

Early entry price activity, 155, 158
Economic events, signalling change, 71
Efficiency, degree of, horizontal and vertical, relationship between, 65–66, 66t
Electrocomponents PLC, daily Market Profile of, 163, 164f
Electronic access, 57
Endings, looking for, 81
Excess(es), 92
  and Novellus Systems, 120–121, 121f
  volume, 117–122
  Volume$, location of, in chart display, 121, 121f
Experience, learning from, 12–13
Extreme, blow off, 115–117
  in Gillette stock, 116f, 116–117
  definition of, 83

Fair value, 8–9
Focused output, 194f, 194–195
Ford, Henry, 187
Ford Motor Company, Market Profile of, 23, 24f
Fundamental information, technical information, and market, 46–47
Funds, Liquidity Data Bank report and, 99, 111–113

Gates, Bill, 187
Global Crossings stock, volume@time output, 107–108, 109t
Greenspan, Alan, 72, 186

Hawkins, Steven B., website of, 116
Hawkins interpretation, 51–213
Horizontal ratio studies, 198
Human behavior, markets and, 127
Human capacity, 153–154

Information, real-time, Chicago Board of Trade and, 45–46
Information revolution, 43–47
Initiating activity, 89–92

Japanese yen, Market Profile of, 53, 55f

Learning, by observation, 33
from experience, 12–13
Life-of-contract high, 69
Liquidity Data Bank, description of, 97
printout of, of 30-year Treasury bonds, 110–111, 111f
report of, 100f
funds and, 99, 112–113
interpretation of, steps in, 108–113, 114f
purpose of, 108
understanding of, 98–101
Lonesome calculation, 198
Long-term Capital, 185–186
Lucent Technologies, Market Profile of, 34f, 35

Macro profile, 68
Market(s), activity of, determination of place in, 148
developmental phase of, 71
four steps of, 70–74
minimum trends and, 20
as organized medium, 126–127
at work, 8–13
changing, 37–42
conditions of, value and, 10
value of stock and, 32
definition of, 125

emerging, opportunities offered by, 186–187
fundamental and technical information and, 46–47
human behavior and, 127
in early 1960s, 31
in nonrandom state, on floor information and, 113
in 1970s, 40–41
internal time clock of, 73–74, 77–78
locations of, 125–126
natural organization of, 44–46
price/time usage in, normal distribution of, 25
price to stop, trading to, 71, 77, 81f
purpose of, 131–132
reading of, and not reacting, 153
responsive, success in, 32–33
services provided by, 126
speed of movement of, Steidlmayer distribution and, 137–138
Steidlmayer theory of, 125–129
theory of, 32
time frames in, 128–129
trader as objective observer of, 139–140
trends of, determination of, 148
types of auctions in, 126–127
vertical expansion of, 76
Market Activity Units, directional arrows, 201, 202f
Market development, six things in, 127
Market discipline, 141
emotions and, studying of, 141–142
improvement of skills in, 143
study of trades of day in, 141
traders and, 142–143
Market information source, elements necessary for, 126
Market Profile, 21, 147
and ordinary technical analysis, compared, 56

Market Profile (*Continued*)
  as normal distribution curve, 58,
    59f
  as technical information, 47
  basic principles of, 56–57
  chart, reading of, 57–59
  creation of, 73
  graphics, 21–23, 22f, 23f
  graphing of, 51
  in conjunction with observations
    and experiences, 95
  market-imposed timeframe and, 66
  of neutral day, 63, 63f
  of nontrend day, 60, 61f
  of normal day, 62, 62f
  of normal variation day, 61, 61f
  of running profile neutral day, 64,
    65f
  of trend day, 62, 62f
  reading information communicated
    by, 56
  spread between bund and bobl, 92f,
    93–94, 94f
  spread between Nasdaq and
    Standard and Poor, 93, 95f
  standard criteria, Dow futures
    contract graphed to, 52–53, 54f
  understanding of, 51–96
  uses of, 94
Market Profile+, 199
Market Profile display, 186–188
Market Profile flow chart pyramid,
  187f, 187–188
Market time, 70, 72, 189–191
Market time database, 189–191, 190f
Marketplace, common laws of,
  35–36
Mattel Inc., daily bar chart of, 120,
  120f
  excess in spreadsheet of, 118–119,
    119f
MD_Trader™ display, 205–206, 205f,
  208–209, 210f
Minimum trend(s), and market
  activity, 19
  charting of, 21–28, 22f

definition of, 19–20
  grouped to form bell curve, 20f,
    20–21
  John Schultz and, 19–21, 58,
    67–68, 127
  profile, hypothetical, 27, 27f, 28f
Minus development, 176, 177, 178
Money, ways to make in trading, 186
Municipal Bond Index, traded on
  Chicago Board of Trade, daily
  profile display of, 75–76, 76f

Narrow-range days, 41–42
Note contract, 5-year, on floor
  information numbers and,
  113–114, 114f
Novellus Systems, excess and,
  120–121, 121f
  zero line, 122–123, 123f

Observation, and understanding for
  results, 6
  learning by, 33
On floor information, buying, 102
  description of, 97–98
  display, of 30-year Treasury bond,
    104f, 104–105
    referenced, daily profile display
      of, 155–157, 156f
    standard, 103f, 103–104
  interpretation of, steps in, 113–114
  numbers, 101, 113, 155–156
    affixed to respective profile,
      157f
  ratio, 101, 102
  selling, 101
  understanding of, 101–105
One-tick scale, 178f, 178–179
Order, and control, secrets of, 6–7
  bell curve and, 18
Order-routing system, 56–57

Page2 information, 193f, 193–194
Parallel activity trading, 159–162
Phelps Dodge Corporation, Market
  Profile of, 22, 23f

Philip Morris, daily bar chart of, 171, 173f
daily Market Profile of, 171, 172f
Price(s), and value, relationship between, 18
as messenger, 153
behavior around, bell curve and, 20
continued erosion of, to downside, 76, 77
early entry activity, 155, 158
series of, in one direction, 71
to attract traders, 9
zone of, 112
Price areas, different, 127–128
Price database, 106
Problems, importance of facing, 5
Product creation, 198–201
Push and pull of participants, 138

Range extension, 85–86
Responsive activity, 89–92
Retracement, 71
Risk, control of, 150
Rosenthal, Les, 43–44
Royal Dutch Petroleum, daily bar chart of, 92, 93f
Rubin, Robert, 186

Schultz, John, and minimum trend, 19–21, 58, 67–68, 127
Sears stock, volume@time output, 107, 108f
Self, looking beyond, 7–8
Selling below value, 90, 91f
Selling tail, 83
Single prints, 171–176, 174f
Sony Corporation, Market Profile of, 90, 91f
Soybeans, July, display of, 73–74, 74f
Spreadsheet, of Mattel Inc., excess in, 118–119, 119f
Stand-alone strategy, 163
Standard deviation, concept of, 58
Steidlmayer, J. Peter, breaking in as trader, 30–31

Chicago Board of Trade and, 28, 29
college years of, 15–28
early lessons of, 3–13
in Chicago, 29–36
Steidlmayer bar chart with DMR overlay, 195–196, 196f
Steidlmayer distribution, 131–138
and speed of market movement, 137–138
illustration of, 132f, 133–136, 135f, 136f
versus normal distribution, 132–134, 133f
Steidlmayer Method, 3–47
Steidlmayer theory of markets, 125–129
Stock, value of, market conditions and, 32
Stops, 150–151
Success, equation for, 32, 39, 143
Symmetrical neutral day, 167

Technical analysis, ordinary, and Market Profile, compared, 56
Technical information, fundamental information, and market, 46–47
Time clock, internal, of market, 73–75, 78–79
Time/price opportunity(ies), 51–53, 57, 74
composite profile, 77f, 77–78
count, 86
interpretation of, 86–87, 87f, 88f
value area, 89
wide point, 76–77, 79
Timeslots-used matrix, 75–81
Trade(s), anatomy of, 145–180
and limitation of number of contracts traded, 150
methods to improve, 151–152
opportunities for, limiting of, 151
looking for, 147–148
to price to stop market, 71
Trade facilitation, 131
phenomenon of, 33
Trade management, 149

Trade setups, 151–152
Trader(s), as objective observer of
  market, 139–140
 beyond-the-day, 129
 capital-safe, 181
 commodity, 16
  article on, 15
  loss of money by, 19
 continuing education needed by,
  146
 day time frame, 129
 early lessons of, 3–5
 following through on task, 6
 fundamental, 147
 game plan for, 146–151
 generic approach for, 147
 guidelines for, 182–183
 ideal position for, 113
 intuitive, 147
 long- and short-term, exposure and
  excesses and, 33–35
 looking for endings, 81
 market discipline and, 142–143
 opportunity time frame, 129
 price to attract, 9
 requirements for, 181
 sense of price/value relationship
  of, 183
 strategy of, creation of, 149
 successful, elements of, 3
  profile of, 181–183
 systemic thought process of, 147
 technical, 147
 unselfishness of, 8
Trading, compared to football, 145
 day structure, 163–168
 high level of, creation of,
  176–180
 intuitive aspect of, 95
 parallel activity, 159–161
 recognizing opportunities and
  getting edge, 202
 shortest time horizon, 153–154
 technology, and future, 185–214
 use of latest technology for, 203
 ways to make money in, 186

Trading day(s), market-imposed
  timeframe of, 67
 neutral, Market Profile, 63–64, 64f
 nontrend, Market Profile, 61f,
  61–62
 normal, Market Profile, 62f, 62–63
 normal variation, Market Profile,
  61f, 63
 running profile neutral, Market
  Profile, 65f, 65–66
 structure of, matrix of, 66, 66t
 trend, Market Profile, 62f, 63
 types of, 34
Trading program, creation of, 18
Trading Technologies International,
  new automated order tool, 209
 X_RISK™, 212
 X_TRADER® of, 205, 206
Trading volume, charting of, formula
  for, 25
Trapped money, 88–89
Treasury bond(s), 30-year, daily bar
  chart of, 104, 104f, 111, 111f
  Liquidity Data Bank printout of,
   109–110, 110f
  on floor information display of,
   103f, 103–104
  traded at Chicago Board of
   Trade, 69
  daily Market Profile display of,
   164, 165f, 166f, 166–167
Tribune Company, extremes and, 84,
  84f
Trust, and freedom, 4
Two-month profile, 69, 70f

Understanding, and observation, for
  results, 6
United States note, 10-year, 26f, 27

Value, and market conditions, 10
 buying below, 90
 price and, relationship between, 18
 selling below, 90, 91f
Value area, calculation of, 89
 definition of, 89

Volume database, 106
Volume excess, 117–123
Volume$ excess, location of, in chart
    display, 121–122, 122f
Volume studies, 153–154
Volume@time, 97, 98
  information generated from
      Capflow32, 106, 107f, 114–115

interpretation of, steps in,
    114–115
output measurement of, 115
understanding of, 105–107

Zero line, 123
  Novellus Systems, 123, 124f
Zone of prices, 112